Process *and* Politics in Library Research

A MODEL FOR COURSE DESIGN

Deborah Fink

American Library Association

CHICAGO AND LONDON 1989

Cover art by Harriett Banner

Designed by Charles Bozett

Composed by Point West, Inc.,
in Baskerville on a Quadex
5000/Compugraphic 8600
digital typesetting system

Printed on 50-pound Glatfelter, a
pH-neutral stock, and bound in
10-point Carolina cover stock by
Versa Press, Inc.

The paper used in this publication meets the minimum requirements of American National
Standard for Information Sciences—Permanence of Paper for Printed Library Materials,
ANSI Z39.48-1984. ∞

Library of Congress Cataloging-in-Publication Data

Fink, Deborah, 1949–
    Process and politics in library research : a model for course design / by Deborah Fink.
        p.   cm.
    Includes index.
    ISBN 0-8389-0519-6
    1. Bibliography—Methodology—Study and teaching (Higher) 2. Research—
    Methodology—Study and teaching (Higher)   3. College students—Library orientation.
    4. Libraries and students.   I. Title.
    Z711.2.F53   1989
    011.4′2′0711—dc20   89-14924

This book is dedicated to my parents,
who creatively nurtured me, and my husband,
with whom I lovingly share critical thought

Contents

Acknowledgments

The course described in this book has been evolving since 1977, when I was in library school and a teaching assistant for the University of California at Los Angeles (UCLA) library skills course. I adapted the syllabus for that class to teach a similar course during my first professional position at the University of Dubuque (Iowa). Since joining the library faculty at the University of Colorado, Boulder (UCB), in 1980, I have worked with other librarians there to develop its longstanding two-credit course; the first prepackaged course syllabus was available in spring 1982. In January 1985, I was inspired during a weekend workshop for faculty women to revise the course to reflect my commitment to feminist ideals; I also read John Naisbett's *Megatrends*, and the result was a paradigm for information processing, highlighting the politics of information, which I presented in a paper at the 1986 Association of College and Research Libraries conference. Bettina (Tina) MacAyeal of ALA Books heard that presentation and suggested a book, which I initiated on sabbatical in fall 1986 when I began to focus on creative problem solving and active learning.

All of this is by way of expressing my appreciation to those who contributed to the rewarding experience of writing this book: the UCLA Graduate School of Library and Information Science, which offered me the opportunity to be a teaching assistant; the UCB librarians who taught sections of Bibliography 301 and contributed to its course manual—especially Susan Anthes, who is always ready to experiment and who read the manuscript chapter by chapter; Charlotta Hensley for her willingness to shape her guest lecture into a chapter during a time of extraordinary demands; the University of Colorado, Boulder, and its University Libraries for professional development support; Tina MacAyeal for suggesting the book and her enthusiastic responses; Bart Greenberg for his emotional support, intellectual involvement, and undaunted editing; and, of course, the students, who make it all worthwhile by sharing the pleasure and pain of learning.

Introduction

From the perspective of bibliographic education, the concept of an "information society" is very appealing. The appellation itself brings focus to the very substance of librarianship, libraries, and research. That an entire culture and period in time have been so designated attests to the value and significance of information. Widespread use of the term has stimulated general interest in the production and acquisition of information. Teaching librarians can capitalize on this fascination by making it a context for the presentation of library skills.

However, the quantity of and need for information that characterize this society present problems rather than solutions. It is problematical that information permeates society to the level of a glut, making it difficult to discern the valid from the spurious. It is problematical that the complexity, diversity, specialization, and acceleration of this society require incessantly more, and more current, information to function effectively. It is problematical that information is viewed as an end in itself and that the distinction between information and knowledge is increasingly disregarded.

Knowledge may appear to offer more benefit than information does, but knowledge per se is static: it is not readily permuted for growth. It is no longer appropriate for students to learn merely a collection of knowledge, which, given the information explosion, may rapidly become obsolete. Rather, students must learn the process of acquiring, evaluating, and assimilating information as needed. But information is not an end goal; information is a tool for understanding, action, knowledge, and growth—i.e., learning. Because learning is essentially dynamic and suggests a solution rather than posing problems, it offers a more compelling label for this era in the United States.

The term *learning society* was suggested by the National Commission on Excellence in Education in *A Nation at Risk*, which states:

> At the heart of such a society is the commitment to a set of values and to a system of education that affords all members the opportunity to stretch their minds to full capacity, from early childhood through adulthood, learning more as the world itself changes. Such a society has as a basic foundation the idea that education is important not only because of what it contributes to one's career goals but also because of the value it adds to the general quality of one's life.[1]

Librarians have a key role in the learning society. Libraries, of course, are repositories of accumulated information and recorded knowledge. Growing collections require complex, varied, and flexible systems for storage and retrieval. Teaching librarians must prepare students to use these rapidly changing systems with confidence. We can no longer simply emphasize specific sources or provide static information: *we must teach the process of lifelong learning.*

This book presents the facets of bibliographic instruction in new light. Rather than the library, the information learning society is the context for the research process. The central skills are not library use, but creative problem solving and critical evaluation. The focus is less on particular subject content than on discovering latent issues and fresh approaches. The methodology includes the lecture, but primarily as a stimulus for active learning.

Active Learning

The function of teaching is to provide an environment which stimulates learning. Learning is a result not of passively hearing and remembering but of becoming engaged with information and transmuting it into knowledge and growth. The goal of this course is to engender active learners: students who will venture beyond classroom and classroom boundaries to deliberately seek and critically evaluate information for the rest of their lives.

David Kolb defines learning as "the process whereby knowledge is created through the transformation of experience."[2] Kolb's premises of active learning, derived primarily from John Dewey, Kurt Lewin, and Jean Piaget, are described by David Jaques:

1. We learn best when we are personally involved in the learning experience.
2. Knowledge of any kind has more significance when we learn it through our own initiative, insight and discovery.
3. Learning is best when we are committed to aims that we have been involved in setting, when our participation with others is valued and when there is a supportive framework in which to learn.[3]

In the recent spate of reports on undergraduate education, active learning is viewed as imperative.[4] For example, a study group of the National Institute of Education set forth twenty-seven recommendations for improving undergraduate education because:

The United States must become a nation of educated people. Its citizens should be knowledgeable, creative, and open to ideas. Above all, they should learn how to learn so they can pursue knowledge throughout their lives and assist their children in the same quest.[5]

The study group's report, explicitly titled *Involvement in Learning*, asserts two fundamental principles for educational excellence:

1. The amount of student learning and personal development associated with any educational program is directly proportional to the quality and quantity of student involvement in that program.
2. The effectiveness of any educational policy or practice is directly related to the capacity of that policy or practice to increase student involvement in learning.[6]

Students learn best when they are not the passive receivers of information but the active creators of knowledge, as stated in an ancient oriental proverb: "Tell me, I forget. Show me, I remember. Involve me, I understand." This fact is especially apparent in library instruction. Lectures on the use of library sources, even demonstrations, are meaningless until students use the sources for themselves. The principles of research are equally opaque until applied. The classroom experience is important not only for imparting information but also for stimulating interest in the material presented so that students are motivated to apply the information. And, as Kolb asserts and undergraduate pedagogy confirms, students are motivated to learn when they are active participants in creating the classroom experience.

A Model for Library Course Design

PROCESS AND POLITICS IN LIBRARY RESEARCH is intended for the professional librarian who, whether developing a new library skills course or revising an existing course, is seeking a dynamic presentation to engage students and transmit enthusiasm for research. This book provides concepts to cover and issues to raise (though not necessarily resolve) in order to stimulate critical thinking. There are many ways to structure class sessions to promote critical thinking through active learning. Here, discussion questions, individual and small-group activities, and library-based exercises are the primary approaches. Options for a course framework are provided, but the instructor determines the particulars and students should be involved in the selection of alternatives.

Discussions in this book are presented dialectically, i.e., diverging views are offered. For example, weaknesses of access sources as well as their utility are described, not to pronounce judgment or suggest solutions, but to open questions and encourage creative approaches. It is a disservice to students to present library materials as above question or value-free: while sources may provide answers, they do not necessarily do so from a neutral position. No compilation of information is value-free—if we expect students to seek and use information critically, we must present the tools of the search critically.

How to Use This Model: Unit Design

PROCESS AND POLITICS IN LIBRARY RESEARCH is a guide for creating learning opportunities in an academic course for undergraduate student researchers (variously referred to as the undergraduate, student, or researcher). Each chapter includes an overview of the subject; samples of learning objectives, class discussion questions, in-class activities, and take-home exercises; and suggested reading.

OVERVIEW

Each chapter's overview is offered as a basis for determining unit content and issues, but not as a lecture text. Intended only to suggest key points and not to be comprehensive or definitive, the overview is provided as a framework for development. Read each overview as an introduction to the topic; then use the most appealing references cited in the overviews for more in-depth coverage and additional material consistent with your individual interests and goals. Next, select or develop student learning objectives for each unit, as well as concepts and applications for each objective.

CONCEPTS

Each chapter or instructional unit is topical and not indicative of class time or emphasis. Some chapters are easily covered in one class session (such as "Creative Problem Solving"), while others will require two or more sessions (such as "Computerized Information Access"). Select concepts to cover and then decide how much class time to spend on each unit.

Perhaps the most difficult aspect of lesson planning is keeping the content to a minimum. The best advice here is that *less is more*. It is a grave disservice to saturate or overwhelm students, who can absorb only so much in a class session; students may embrace a few concepts presented well, but are likely to reject a multitude of ideas presented superficially. The number of concepts presented should be kept to a minimum also to allow full development through active learning. Skill applications must be selected and implemented as carefully and consistently as concepts.

APPLICATIONS

Each chapter includes sample discussion questions, which are intended to suggest further ideas.[7] Discussion questions are a simple but powerful technique for stimulating active learning. When thoughtfully developed and integrated into a class session, questions typically engage students, whether they show it or not: when questions are posed, the mind almost reflexively seeks answers. Even if their thoughts are not articulated, students will be more actively involved with the material when a discussion is taking place than when they are simply listening to a lecture.

Discussion questions can be used to lead into, break up, or conclude a class session; they can also substitute for a significant portion of a lecture. In response to questions, students will usually cover many of the points that the instructor planned to include in the lecture. You can then simply fill in, clarify, or summarize, giving students the opportunity to acknowledge what they already know. It is more interesting and lively to talk with students, responding to points they raise, than to unilaterally talk at a class: the interaction is well worth any loss of organization or material.

Active learning is also effectively achieved by asking students to respond in writing to questions. A five-minute interlude in which students record their responses to a question (to be shared orally or not) varies the pace and impels involvement in a nonthreatening way. Another technique is to distribute questions in advance of the class session; students are more likely to be prepared for class discussion when they know what questions will be addressed. Lists of questions are also useful for focusing reading assignments. As a supplement to take-home exercises, a list of questions provides alternative phrasing and focused emphasis on the assignment (see sample in-class discussion questions distributed with the take-home assignment on background sources in chapter 4).

Each chapter also includes sample in-class activities and take-home exercises. Here again, the examples are suggestive only and intended to stimulate additional ideas.[8] Taking part in brief in-class activities involves the individual student as effectively as answering questions orally or in writing. Cooperative or small-group activities structure interaction that is even more dynamic and therefore conducive to learning. The sample take-home exercises provide opportunities to apply and fully experience the concepts and skills presented in class. Many of the take-home exercises can be completed by students working in pairs or small groups as well as individually. The take-home exercises may be used with a single course research topic or various assigned or selected topics. When using a consistent topic, many of the exercises work well cumulatively over the course of a term.

INSTRUCTIONAL FORMAT

In order to continuously make explicit the coherence of the entire course and to structure selected concepts and applications with a beginning, middle, and end, the following format is suggested for class sessions.[9]

> *Review*: Begin each class session with a brief review of the previous session and the development of the course to date, in order to create a transition to the new topic and integrate it into the course.
> *Recall and Relate*: Bring to the students' minds some previous experience or attitude or information that relates to the day's topic. This reminder provides a personal connection and active transition to the topic. For example, I like to begin the session on classification

in chapter 9 by asking how classification is used in our daily lives. It usually takes several minutes before students realize, with an "aha," that most kitchens, closets, etc., conform to some system of classification.

Explore: Present new material.

Experience: Provide opportunities to apply concepts in active learning experiences.

Figure 1 is a learning plan format to facilitate this process.

Topic:

Number of class sessions/amount of time:

Concepts:

Applications:

Instructional Format:

    Review:

    Recall/Relate:

    Explore:

    Explain:

Figure 1. Learning plan

Course Design

In addition to a plan for each unit and class session, the entire course must be organized with a course outline or schedule with due dates, exercises, reading assignments, course projects, and final exam.[10]

To develop a course outline, first sequence the instructional units. The chapters in this book demonstrate one possible order. This order has a logic to it, but many variations are possible and may be preferred for a variety of reasons. For example, I have introduced students to computers with a hands-on word-processing lab early in the term so that they could apply that skill throughout the semester. I have also presented newspapers or government publications earlier in the semester in order to introduce the concept of information politics by discussing issues related to the First Amendment or access to government information. I always schedule several field trips (highly recommended), for example to the audiovisual and special collections departments, and sometimes the sequence is dependent on the availability of other librarians.

Once the order of the units has been determined, decide how many class sessions to spend on each unit based on your objectives for the unit. Be sure to allow enough time for in-class activities, some of which may take most or all of a class session depending on the length of class periods. Next, select or develop take-home exercises and add them to the schedule.

An important consideration in sequencing is the distribution of the work load based on selected take-home exercises and due dates. One way to avoid crowding due dates in the second half of the term is to schedule some units that include take-home exercises as early as possible in the term. I cover a miscellany of reference works (see chapter 2, "Reference Tools") by the third week of the semester in order to schedule an exercise as soon as possible and get students working with easier sources that they can explore effectively without a specific research topic.

You may choose to include readings as part of the course work. Reading assignments should be included in the course schedule. I have compiled a course manual consisting of lists of sources (with location and call number) for relevant units, as well as library handouts and miscellaneous articles and excerpts. I also assign a trade research paper guide (one that includes a style manual) as a supplement to the course manual and for an alternative approach to some of the subjects covered.[11]

The nature and amount of course work will, of course, be proportional to the number of course credit hours. For a one credit hour course, take-home exercises may be sufficient. For a two credit hour course, a course project might be required in addition to, or building on, the exercises. If the course earns three credit hours, a final examination may be given in addition to the exercises and project (see figure 5 for a sample final essay question).

I have used several different course projects. One approach is a pathfinder, outlined in figure 2. Students select a research topic early in the term to use for all the exercises. The sources examined in each exercise are then compiled as a pathfinder, which is intended to serve as an organizational framework for what is learned about researching the topic as well as a model for future search strategies. I have also allowed students to select from several course project options or to develop their own miniproject. The course project, which is more formal and includes specific guidelines, is shown in figure 3. The miniproject imposes fewer expectations and provides more personal choice; a sample appears in figure 4. If these project options are made available, I require a project proposal by midterm, when I often schedule individual consultations. I also require students to develop the criteria (subject to negotiation and my approval) that I will use to evaluate the project. This criteria development typically proves difficult but enlightening for students.

Two other activities that I have found particularly successful are small-group presentations and personal journals. Working in small groups, students get to know each other and establish a pattern of dynamic interaction that contributes to a more lively, stimulating class. (The suggested take-home and in-class assignment in chapter 1 is very effective for stimulating cooperation as well as critical thinking and is recommended for implementation early in the term.) In addition, students can be asked to maintain a personal journal throughout the course, in which they record their responses to class sessions, readings, assignments, and their research topic. This journal provides students an opportunity to acknowledge and affirm the variety of emotions they experience as a part of the research process. The affective aspect of research is rarely addressed explicitly, although feelings color and regulate much of the process.[12]

Topic

A limited subject will work best. The topic should be typed in all capital letters and centered one and one-half inches from the top of the page (do not use the section heading "topic").

Scope

A concise, explanatory, factual statement to define and delimit your topic, this note should be derived but not directly quoted from authoritative sources.

Example:

Topic: Child Abuse: The Generation Cycle

Scope: Child abuse is the intentional harm (physical or emotional) to a child by a parent or guardian. When children who have been beaten grow up to abuse their own children, this is known as the generation cycle.

Introduction

List an article in a reference work, periodical, or book that will provide a brief overview or general introduction to the topic.

Encyclopedias and Dictionaries

This section may be combined with the introduction, or encyclopedias and dictionaries may be excluded in some cases. You may wish to cite specific articles or suggest key terms defined in the dictionary. Five or fewer relevant titles should be included.

Guidebooks

If a guidebook is available, the value and use of this tool should be emphasized in an annotation. For example, highlight features that will be particularly useful in researching the topic and list appropriate chapters or sections.

Access Terms for the Online and Card Catalogs

Prioritize the best headings to look under in the subject card catalog. In a separate column, list additional terms (not established subject headings) that can also be used to access materials in the Online Public Access Catalog.

Example:

Card Catalog Subject Headings	Additional Public Access Catalog Search Term
CHILD ABUSE	CHILD NEGLECT
CHILD ABUSE— CASE STUDIES	
CRUELTY TO CHILDREN	
CHILD WELFARE	
CHILDREN—LAW	
CHILDREN'S RIGHTS	

Key Texts

List the classic and definitive works available, especially recent ones. Appropriate titles for this section will be cited repeatedly in bibliographies and articles. If you identify key texts not available on campus, be sure to indicate their unavailability in an annotation. This section should be limited to no more than ten texts, all of which should be briefly annotated.

Bibliographies
You can include subject-specific bibliographies or general bibliographies (e.g., *Subject Guide to Books in Print*) for discovering what has been published on the topic. When referring to a general bibliography, suggest the most relevant subject headings to use.

Indexes
Periodical and newspaper indexes should be listed in priority order. Give the full title and list the most pertinent subject headings for each index.

Key Articles
List here periodical and newspaper articles on your topic that are particularly timely or informative. This section should be limited to no more than ten articles, all of which should be annotated. Indicate in the annotation if an article is not available on campus.

Other Sources
Depending upon your topic, a section on other sources may be particularly important or excluded altogether. Use it to cite relevant sources in computer databases, government publications, review sources, biographical tools, etc.

Summarizing Comments
Discuss in a single paragraph problems a user might encounter when researching this topic. Points to consider include: more literature available on topic than can be used; very little available in books, journals, etc.; available information too pe-

ripheral; many of the sources in foreign languages; nonavailability of sources on campus; general tips for an effective search.

General Guidelines
1. The final copy of your pathfinder must be typed.
2. Cite all entries according to the style manual.
3. The section headings should be in all capitals. In some cases you may wish to precede entries in sections with a lead-in phrase when the section heading needs explanation.
4. In some sections you may list only one item: in those cases singularize the heading. For example, if you list only one bibliography, change the heading from "bibliographies" to "bibliography."
5. Arrange the entries in each section alphabetically, or provide an explanation of the arrangement if it is not alphabetical.
6. Note that all pathfinders will *not* necessarily have entries for each section outlined above. Some topics, for example, will not have guidebooks or bibliographies available.
7. Examine all items to be included if they are available on campus.
8. Use the following criteria as guidelines for selecting entries (especially in the key texts and key articles sections):
   A. relevancy to topic
   B. recency of information
   C. frequency of appearance in bibliographies
   D. availability on campus.

Figure 2. Sample pathfinder format and guidelines

As the culmination of what you learn about your topic and access to information, develop and submit a course project. By choosing a topic and project format, you may make the course as personally relevant and interesting
as you wish. Your project is expected to demonstrate mastery of the following skills: creative problem solving, search strategy development and
follow-through, documentation and evaluation of sources, assimilation and
application of information. Your project proposal is due at midterm. Following are four project formats from which to choose.

Bibliographic Essay
In a four- to twelve-page essay, analyze the access to information on your
topic. Describe your strategy and vocabulary control and assess the relevance and value of specific sources, which must be cited perfectly in the
text of your essay. Discuss the availability and politics of information on your
topic.

Annotated Bibliography
Compile your exercise results as a list of sources on your topic. The list may
be arranged as an alphabetical bibliography or as a categorized pathfinder
(e.g., background sources, access sources, periodical articles, books, government publications, etc.). The bibliography must include citations in perfect style and an annotation describing and evaluating each entry.

Research Paper
Write a five- to ten-page paper on your topic, including endnotes and a list,
in perfect style, of sources consulted. The paper should demonstrate the
thoroughness of your search strategy as well as your ability to select essential and well-balanced information, and present it concisely.

Oral Report
Make a formal presentation to the class on your topic and access to your
topic (see description under Bibliographic Essay). Prior to the presentation,
submit an outline and list of sources (cited perfectly) to the instructor.

Project Proposal Format
Name:

Topic:

Type of Project:

Criteria to be used by instructor to evaluate project:

Intended grade:

Figure 3. Sample course project options

In addition to the course exercises, develop and submit a course miniproject. Use creative problem-solving techniques (e.g., brainstorming and visual representation) to determine the nature and structure of your own project. This assignment gives you the opportunity to make the course as personally relevant and interesting (maybe even as fun) as you wish. The project may or may not be related to your course research topic. Two or more individuals may work on the same project together.

Requirements
Your project must demonstrate mastery of the following skills:
> Creative problem solving
> Search strategy development and follow-through
> Documentation and evaluation of sources
> Assimilation and application of information.

Possible Formats (you are not limited to this list)
Research essay	Computer project
Pathfinder	Presentation
Bibliography	Debate
Research component of	Performance
paper for another class	Artwork
Journal	Class activity

Proposal
Your name:

Names of others working on the project:

Description of project:

Timeline or table:

How project will demonstrate mastery of skills:

Criteria to be used by instructor to evaluate project:

Intended grade:

Figure 4. Sample miniproject guidelines

Think back over all the steps you have taken in your search for information on your topic. Discuss your thoughts and reflections about the search process you have engaged in.

This essay is open book: you may refer to your notes, course manual, or research paper guide. You will be graded on inclusion of all steps in the research process, as well as the clarity and thoughtfulness of your analysis of the entire process.

Cover the following two areas in your essay.

1. Focus on how each step of the search has functioned to provide access to information sources. You may want to comment on why you encountered difficulties at particular points in the search, as well as your successes. Also address your experience of how library systems and reference sources promote and hinder access to information, as well as the political nature of the information sources themselves (i.e., periodicals, newspapers, books, government publications, etc.).

2. What would you do differently now to research the same topic—i.e., now that you have experienced a generalized search strategy, how would you better organize an approach to your particular topic?

Figure 5. Sample final in-class essay

Benefits of the Credit Course

The credit course as a format for library education has been challenged in terms of both efficiency (it is librarian labor intensive for comparatively few students) and effectiveness (students are not trained at time of need). While I do not deny such concerns, my own experience confirms the value of this approach. Certainly the course requires a lot of time and energy, but my professional knowledge and commitment have deepened as a result. I can think of no better way to learn and keep up with a reference collection or know well the students we serve or continuously freshen one's professional perspective than by developing a course and relating to a group of students over time. Another benefit is the shared experience with departmental faculty and enhanced academic status.

One drawback of teaching library use at time of need (i.e., the standard guest lecture approach) is that students are so focused on their need—they feel inconvenienced to bother with library skills in order to accomplish the "real" task of writing a report. Whereas, the credit course provides an opportunity for students to view library research as intrinsically useful and complementary to other endeavors, such as writing a report, advancing in one's occupation, or pursuing continuing education. The value of offering skills and motivation for lifelong learning is undeniable; the teaching librarian has an ideal opportunity to fulfill this need in the learning society.

Notes and Suggested Reading

1. U.S. National Commission on Excellence in Education, *A Nation at Risk: The Imperative for Educational Reform: A Report to the Nation and the Secretary of Education* (Washington, D.C.: Govt. Print. Off., pp. 13–14.

2. David A. Kolb, *Experiential Learning: Experience as the Source of Learning and Development* (Englewood Cliffs, N.J.: Prentice-Hall, 1984), p. 38.

3. David Jaques, *Learning in Groups* (London: Croom Helm, 1984), p. xiii.

4. More than fifty publications are listed in a bibliography of recent reports on undergraduate education: "Report on Reports: What They Say about Teaching at the College Level," *College Teaching* 35:147–151 (Fall 1987). See also a 1988 task group report calling for a revitalization of general education: Association of American Colleges Task Group on General Education, *A New Vitality in General Education: Planning, Teaching, and Supporting Effective Liberal Learning* (Washington, D.C.: Assoc. of Amer. Colleges, 1988).

5. National Institute of Education, Study Group on the Conditions of Excellence in American Higher Education, *Involvement in Learning: Realizing the Potential of American Higher Education* (Washington, D.C.: Govt. Print. Off., 1984), p. 2.

6. Ibid., p. 19.

7. For more information, see Thomas P. Kasulis, "Questioning," in *The Art and Craft of Teaching*, ed. Margaret Morganroth Gullette (Cambridge, Mass.: Harvard Univ. Pr., 1984), pp. 38–48, and William M. Welty, "Discussion Method Teaching: How to Make It Work," *Change* 21: 41–49 (July/August 1989).

8. For background see David W. Johnson and Roger T. Johnson, *Learning Together and Alone: Cooperative, Competitive, and Individualistic Learning*, 2nd ed. (Englewood Cliffs, N.J.: Prentice-Hall, 1987).

9. Inspired by Marilla D. Svinicki and Barbara A. Schwartz, *Designing Instruction for Library Users: A Practical Guide* (New York: Dekker, 1988). These authors apply the principles of learning theory and instructional design to library instruction and adapt Kolb's model of the experiential learning cycle for sequencing instruction. Their series of charts for selecting learning objectives, teaching methods, and evaluation are also useful.

10. See especially Mignon S. Adams and Jacquelyn M. Morris, *Teaching Library Skills for Academic Credit* (Phoenix, Ariz.: Oryx, 1985); also Anne K. Beaubien, Sharon A. Hogan, and Mary W. George, *Learning the Library: Concepts and Methods for Effective Bibliographic Instruction* (New York: Bowker, 1982), pp. 199–216, and Beverly Renford and Linnea Hendrickson, *Bibliographic Instruction: A Handbook* (New York: Neal-Schuman, 1980), pp. 121–149.

11. I have used Kate L. Turabian, *Student's Guide for Writing College Papers*, 3rd ed. (Chicago: Univ. of Chicago Pr., 1976); James D. Lester, *Writing Research Papers: A Complete*

Guide, 5th ed. (Glenview, Ill.: Scott, Foresman, 1987); and Audrey J. Roth, *The Research Paper: Process, Form, and Content*, 6th ed. (Belmont, Calif.: Wadsworth, 1989).

12. Although her research focuses on high-school students, see Carol Collier Kuhlthau, "Developing a Model of the Library Search Process: Cognitive and Affective Aspects," *RQ* 28:232–242 (Winter 1988), and Carol Collier Kuhlthau, *Teaching the Library Research Process: A Step-by-Step Program for Secondary School Students* (West Nyack, N.Y.: Center for Applied Research in Education, 1985).

Chapter *1*

Critical Thinking in the
Information Society

The current unprecedented quantity of and need for information are both the hallmark and the challenge of the information age. In this complex, diversified, and specialized society, citizens must make choices based upon information. And information is generated, packaged, and distributed in a variety and at a rate that make its presence a largely unchallenged element of our daily lives. The very prevalence of information in our society may deter potential users or lead them to the misconception that what is readily available is all that is needed; in fact, much of what is readily available is merely "junk information," the parallel of junk mail and junk food.[1]

Information can be exploited for power or appropriated for empowerment. Influence may be exerted over others by withholding information, selecting only information that supports a particular view, or releasing a flood of information to deliberately confuse and obscure an issue. The ability to access and critically evaluate information is essential for taking action, whether it is in the realm of personal development, professional advancement, or social change. Increasingly, the empowered in this society are those able to transmute information into learning and growth.

Information and the Information Explosion

Technology and information are the primary elements of change in today's society. Since Daniel Bell proclaimed "The Coming of Post-

Portions of this chapter were originally published in the author's chapter, "Information, Technology, and Library Research," in *Conceptual Frameworks for Bibliographic Education: Theory into Practice*, eds. Mary Reichel and Mary Ann Ramey (Littleton, Colo.: Libraries Unlimited, 1987), pp. 24–35.

Industrial Society" in 1973, popular futurist authors have dramatized the effects and significance of current social shifts. In *The Third Wave*, Alvin Toffler depicts civilization awash in a transformation comparable to the industrialization of agricultural society. He claims that "what is happening is not just a technological revolution but the coming of a whole new civilization...." And he maintains that, "For Third Wave civilization, the most basic raw material of all—and one that can never be exhausted—is information...."[2] His vision is reinforced by John Naisbett's delineation of ten "megatrends," including the arrival of the "information society" as "an economic reality."[3]

These authors present a compelling image of an egalitarian, problem-solving future, with a key role for information professionals and a better life for all because of the capacities of computers. A thought-provoking and sobering counterpoint to this picture is Theodore Roszak's *The Cult of Information*. In short, Roszak views the computer as a threat to learning, thinking, privacy, and democracy, and he attacks the glowing new concept of information:

> The word [information] has received ambitious, global definitions that make it all good things to all people. Words that come to mean everything may finally mean nothing; yet their very emptiness may allow them to be filled with a mesmerizing glamour. The loose but exuberant talk we hear on all sides these days about the "information economy," the "information society," is coming to have exactly that function. These often-repeated catch phrases and cliches are the mumbo jumbo of a widespread public cult.[4]

What, then, is "information," and why has it come to be viewed as a national resource? One description of information states:

> In its smallest and most essential form, information can be regarded as a sensory signal, a fact, or a feeling that can be perceived or communicated. We continually receive information— whether or not it is processed further, either consciously or unconsciously. Moreover, information *is* information whether or not it is at the moment retrievable. Information need only have the potential for retrieval.[5]

Harlan Cleveland identifies "the inherent characteristics of information" that qualify it as a "resource."[6] He observes that information actually expands as it is used. Information also leaks, and the more it spreads, the more it increases. When shared, information remains available to the giver as well as the receiver. Information is not resource-hungry and, in fact, increasingly substitutes for capital, labor, and physical materials. Information is also readily transported.

A few statistics attest to the reality of the information "explosion." According to a "Study Report on the Feasibility of a World Science Information System" sponsored by UNESCO in 1971,

> It took until 1750 for man's knowledge at the time of Christ to double. The second doubling was completed 150 years later in 1900. The fourth doubling of all man's knowledge took place in the decade of the 1950s. Looked at another way, technology has multiplied by ten every 50 years for over 2800 years. In 1950, there were one million scientists and engineers in the world; in 1900 there were were 100,000; in 1850, 10,000; and in 1800, 1000.[7]

UNESCO's *Statistical Yearbook* lists, for 1970, more than 2.5 million scientists and engineers globally; that total exceeded 3 million by 1975, and more than 3.5 million by 1980.[8]

Naisbett has determined that between 6,000 and 7,000 scientific articles are written daily, and scientific and technological information increases 13 percent annually, or doubles every 5.5 years. He anticipated that the rate would jump to 40 percent per year, doubling every twenty months.[9]

Advances in electronic technologies have been no less dramatic:

> It took over 5 million years to get from spoken language to writing, about 5,000 years from writing to printing, and 500 years from printing to radio, telephone, film and television. It took only 50 years from the formative period of television to the demonstration of videodiscs, and now [1985] it is about 5 years since the advent of personal computers.[10]

Blaise Cronin enumerates the impacts of information technology. Information, he maintains, is amplified by the increasing capacity to store, access, and transmit data. McLuhan's vision of a global electronic village appears feasible. Furthermore, the acceleration of access to information is profoundly affecting decision making and policy formulation in all types of organizations. Despite concerns about the creation of an information elite by the concentration of commercial electronic information, increased individual autonomy and general decentralization are likely. The workplace is also being transformed as employment structures change radically. There are a new general interest in information and a growing trend towards the commercialization of information that used to be provided by government.[11]

Another significant development is the change in the work force from the production of goods to the provision of services, as discussed at length by Bell, who maintains that:

> Industrial society is the coordination of machines and men for the production of goods. Post-industrial society is organized around knowledge, for the purpose of social control and the directing of innovation and change; and this in turn gives rise to new social relationships and new structures which have to be managed politically.[12]

Naisbett notes that the "overwhelming majority of service workers are actually engaged in the creation, processing, and distribution of information." In 1950, about 17 percent of the work force was in "information" occupations; by the early 1980s, over 60 percent of American workers held what Naisbett designates as information jobs.[13] White-collar workers did not outnumber blue-collar workers in the United States until 1956, but by 1967 information workers accounted for about 46 percent of the Gross National Product and more than 53 percent of income earned.[14]

Skill in accessing and evaluating information, then, may be useful to students as they take their places in the work force, but, certainly, such skill is critical as they assume the responsibilities of citizenship in this information society. In both professional and public policy contexts, there is clear value in being able to make informed choices. Students can become more discriminating information consumers if they are introduced to "the structure of information." As Elizabeth Frick maintains, "by understanding who generates information, who publishes it, who disseminates and classifies it, how, and for whom, [the researcher] will develop a more subtle grasp of the value and limitations of that information."[15]

An Information Processing Model

Frick's suggestions are the basis of a paradigm for information processing, that is, the many operations that cycle information from communication to dissemination to acquisition and from organization to access, assimilation, and communication.[16]

The paradigm, as shown in figure 6, outlines the functions of authors, publishers, librarians, researchers, and writers. It provides a conceptual framework for organizing and presenting a variety of procedures and issues. It can be used to overview the cycle of information processing, to provide context for any of the stages, and to explore the political dimensions of information. It can also be used to demonstrate current applications of rapidly developing technologies and to project future scenarios.

The stages in the flow of information are explicit in the model, but the politics of information and the role of technology are implicit. Also implicit are those items outside the cycle, such as government documents, in-house publications, and pamphlets and other ephemeral and fugitive materials.

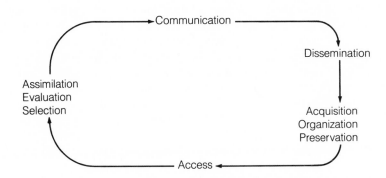

Figure 6. Information processing paradigm

The Politics of Information

Politics is defined here as "promoting a particular interest." In the context of information processing, it includes censorship and selection, which hinder the flow of information; propaganda, which is a distorting device of the author or disseminator; and bias, which is the researcher's conscious or unconscious selection and distortion. Each stage in the cycle of information processing is susceptible to political influences.

Beginning with the communication of information, no author is completely objective, but some harbor a stronger bias than others, whether conscious or not. Even the disciplines with which authors identify themselves influence the perception and communication of information, as each discipline has its own "world view," manifested in the methodology, vocabulary, and literature of the field. The working paradigms of the disciplines determine "acceptable" research and regulate publication.

Propaganda is deliberate distortion through selective or out-of-context publication. It may be created by the author as well as by the disseminator. Even the decisions of whether and how to disseminate information are political choices. The author may limit distribution to colleagues for immediate feedback or seek commercial publication for tenure or other purposes. A publisher will generally accept an item only if it appears to have market value and is consistent with the publisher's public image. Social forces also affect publication. The government and special interest groups have suppressed information, such as the early reports on the detrimental effects of tobacco and the implications of video display terminal research.

Selection for acquisition is, of course, a politically charged process. Bookstores select items that bring a profit; organizations generally select items that support their point of view; and libraries select items that are congruent with their collection development policies. Within the parameters of policies, however, individual librarians make choices based on their own interests and the perceived interests and needs of their constituencies. Often, selections are based on approval plans with major vendors. Materials out of the mainstream may be neglected simply because they are more difficult to identify, acquire, and preserve.[17]

The organization of library materials is less obviously politically charged, but cataloging and classification tools are fraught with controversy: the *Library of Congress Subject Headings* has been labeled sexist, racist, and Anglo-Saxon. Even preservation efforts have political overtones, as decisions are made about what will be preserved, how, and where.

Access to information is the point of connection between the author and the researcher. Access may occur without any intervening steps, but it is most likely to take place where published information has been collected and made available. Access is facilitated by organizational systems and reference sources and services, which make it possible for researchers to identify and locate sources of information. But bibliographic tools are not without politics, both in terms of the items selected for inclusion and their organization. As Frick asserts, "Reference structures both open and close certain information channels, [for example]...the rigidity of certain periodical indexes in regard to subject headings perpetuates certain views of the discipline."[18]

The processing of information by the researcher is prey to political perceptions from the outset. According to West, "The way a problem is stated or conceptualized may exert some influence on the solution and on the pertinent information which is gathered." He also notes that, as research continues, there are "potential distortive effects which emerge from preconceptions about previously gathered information; from prior knowledge; from emotional bias; from group norms; from particular items of information, and restrictions as to the sources of information."[19]

The Impact of New Technologies

The cycle of information processing can also be traced to highlight the impact of new technologies and to clarify the current relationship between conventional and electronic modes of access and manipulation so that researchers can effectively integrate modes during this time of transition.

Word processing makes it easier for writers to prepare their work for submission to a publishing agency. Electronic networks, newsletters, and journals are already enabling writers to communicate without an intermediary publisher, thus eliminating a significant portion of the information-processing cycle. (A dotted line from communication to access might be added to the paradigm in figure 6.) Such developments threaten to create an information elite and have implications for copyright and preservation, but they are increasingly attractive options, given the escalating costs of print journals and the imperative of immediacy in many research areas.

The publishing industry is incorporating computer technologies to enhance standard functions such as typesetting. At the same time, computer and telecommunication advances are giving rise to entirely new aspects of publishing, such as online information retrieval services, electronic journals, electronic document delivery, and electronic bulletin boards and mail systems.

Libraries are using computer technologies to perform routine functions, to generate statistics and reports, to expand storage potential, to take advantage of networking possibilities, to deliver messages and documents, and to provide new forms of access, notably the online catalog. Librarian intermediaries still provide researchers with computer-based access to the online equivalents of printed indexes and other reference sources, but end-user search services are also available in many libraries.

To complete the cycle, traditional methods of organizing research and writing, such as index cards and outlining, are outmoded for writers with access to a personal computer and the growing selection of software for conceptualizing, organizing, writing, editing, and formatting. The effects of these technological developments as well as political influences on the processing of information are recurrent themes throughout this book.

Critical Thinking

Some 100,000 book titles are published annually, more than 1,500 newspapers circulate daily, and over 60,000 general-interest periodicals are available,[20] more than 8,500 radio stations, 1,000 television stations, and 6,500 cable systems broadcast almost ceaselessly.[21] Given this information explosion, it is easy for people to become saturated and difficult for them to become discriminating. Undergraduates may question the value of using the library to find even more information when homes, dorm rooms, campus cafeterias, and sidewalks are littered with it; they may also question the need to evaluate communication by "experts."

The fact that information has been published or produced does not mean it is truthful, authoritative, appropriate, or applicable. "Solid" information is often less readily available than "junk" information. All information arises from frames of reference and is subject to political influences. To make reading, listening, and viewing choices, to advance as a wage-earner, and to develop as a human, each individual must make judgments and choices. Critical thinking is both an attitude and the application of skills by which analytical, integrative judgments and choices are possible. The primary components of critical thinking—critical evaluation and creative problem solving—are covered in subsequent chapters and referred to throughout this book. In this chapter, a definition of the concept is developed.

Robert Ennis, a seminal contributor on the subject, offers a working definition of critical thinking as "reasonable reflective thinking that is focused on deciding what to believe or do."[22] Reviewing the literature on critical thinking up to 1985, Barry Beyer concludes:

> Specialists today appear to agree that critical thinking is the assessing of the authenticity, accuracy and/or worth of knowledge claims and arguments....Critical thinking is unique because it involves careful, precise, persistent and objective *analysis* of any knowledge claim or belief to *judge* its validity and/or worth.[23]

In fact, most writers on the subject describe critical thinking in terms of the analysis and assessment of information. Since the goal of library research is not the mere accumulation of information, but more importantly the evaluation, assimilation, and application of that information, critical thinking is inherent in the research process. In the library literature, Mona McCormick states that critical thinkers:

Identify main issues
Recognize underlying assumptions
Evaluate evidence
Evaluate authorities, people, publications
Recognize bias, emotional appeals, relevant facts, propaganda, generalities, language problems
Question whether facts support conclusions

Question the adequacy of the data
See relationships among ideas
Know their own attitudes and blind spots
Suspend judgment until the search is ended.[24]

Systematically analyzing and questioning in order to evaluate information are one component of critical thinking. Another component is creative problem solving or working integratively from a multiplicity of imaginatively generated perspectives, rather than from predispositions, in order to make judicial choices. Stephen Brookfield maintains that critical thinking is "reflecting on the assumptions underlying our and others' ideas and actions, and contemplating alternative ways of thinking and living." He identifies four components of this process:

1. Identifying and challenging assumptions
2. Developing awareness of context
3. Imagining and exploring alternatives
4. Engaging in reflective skepticism.[25]

Brookfield defines assumptions as:

> ...the seemingly self-evident rules about reality that we use to help us seek explanations, make judgements, or decide on various actions. They are the unquestioned givens that, to us, have the status of self-evident truths. People cannot reach adulthood without bringing with them frameworks of understanding and sets of assumptions that undergrid their decisions, judgements, and actions.[26]

Richard Paul advocates "strong sense" critical thinking, which is built on three capacities: identifying one's own frame of reference, entering into other frames of reference, and reasoning dialectically or multilogically among points of view to synthesize from a variety of perspectives.[27] Thus, critical thinking is both an attitude, or the willingness to examine closely one's own as well as other viewpoints, and a variety of reasoning and imaginative skills.

Critical thinking is necessary throughout the research process. The effective use of any source, from reference tool to newspaper, periodical, book, or government publication, requires evaluation. Procedures, such as selecting a topic, establishing vocabulary control, developing search strategies and tactics, and responding to collected information are enhanced by creative problem solving. At each step of the process, assumptions should be exposed, alternatives identified, and tension created among perspectives in order to release insight.

Students may feel threatened when critical thinking is promoted in the classroom. When this approach is embraced, it enlarges and alters not only perspectives but also lives. Students may feel challenged to a point of discomfort when they can no longer rationalize a protected belief or when an opposing view begins to make sense. They may resent classroom discussions that open questions rather than provide unequivocal answers or that critique sources that students believed were above question. Because of limited exposure to this approach, many students will resist or resent taking responsibility for their own learning. Other students may fervently challenge everything, abandoning old values and committing to new causes.

Some critics of public education, school library materials, and textbooks have challenged the use of materials and methods that "undermine" beliefs and morals. Clearly, this author supports the risks of actively learning critical thinking and perceives such risks as an inherent and vital aspect of living, especially in a society in which information is power. Teaching librarians are encouraged, however, to anticipate and openly discuss their students' responses to and concerns about this approach and its effects on their lives. As Brookfield comments:

> Anyone seeking to promote critical thinking in others should...
> also be bound by an ethical imperative to point out...the potential risks involved in various change efforts that might result
> from this critical scrutiny.[28]

Whether the continuing transition to a computer-based "information society" is viewed as a democratizing and enabling transformation or an insidious subversion of democracy, the ability to access and evaluate information is required to contribute to the current culture of accelerating change, which is perhaps more aptly dubbed the "learning society." This guide places library use in a larger social context to encourage students and teaching librarians to examine information critically and to apply it creatively as a tool for personal development and a force for social change.

Sample Learning Objectives

Concepts to understand:

The contemporary United States as "information society" (or "cult of information").

Information as a resource transforming the work place.

How political and technological forces shape the stages in the cycle of information processing.

Critical thinking both as an attitude and as skill for critical evaluation and creative problem solving.

The function and value of critical thinking.

Skills to apply:

Becoming aware of the daily barrage of information and developing more active and critical responses to it.

Identifying frames of reference and multiple perspectives.

Sample Class Discussion Questions

1. Share a piece of information you acquired today.
2. What is information?
3. List some forms of information you encounter in a typical day.
4. What kinds of decisions do you make based on information?
5. How have electronic technologies and the information explosion changed our society compared to twenty years ago? Compared to fifty years ago? Compared to one hundred years ago?
6. List some information-handling occupations.
7. List the players in the information infrastructure: who are the producers? Disseminators? Collectors and providers? Users?
8. What are the characteristics of information that qualify it as a "resource"?
9. How is information power?
10. Given the transformations from an agrarian to an industrial to an information society, what do you think will be the next major social revolution?
11. Do you agree with Theodore Roszak that our culture has, in fact, become a "cult of information"?
12. What are the stages in the cycle of information processing?
13. How do you define "politics"?
14. What is the difference between selection and censorship?
15. What is "critical thinking"?
16. What is a "frame of reference"?
17. Why is it useful to explore alternative perspectives?
18. Why is critical thinking essential in this society?

19. What are some situations in which you are aware of thinking critically?
20. How do you think critical thinking will be useful in the library research process?

Sample In-Class Activities

1. Students take five or ten minutes to write down their impressions, knowledge, and concerns about the information society. Responses are shared with the class.
2. In small groups, students list the pros and cons of the current mania for computers and information.
3. In small groups, students choose one or more occupations and list the information-handling functions that are a part of these jobs. Groups report back to the class at large.
4. Given a controversial issue, students identify points of view on the subject.

Suggested Take-Home and In-Class Assignment

Students form five small groups. Each group is responsible for one of the five sections in the anthology *Censorship: Opposing Viewpoints*, ed. Terry O'Neill (St. Paul: Greenhaven, 1985). Each group presents a debate on its topic. Students in the audience question the debaters and evaluate the presentation.

Sample Take-Home Exercises

1. Students write a brief essay discussing the characteristics and implications of the information society.
2. Students keep a log for two to three days or one week of all the new information they acquire. For each piece of information, they include the source, write a brief summary of the information, and indicate how they expect it to be of use. They also record the choices they make that require information and how they acquired that information.
3. For the next two weeks, as they read, watch, or listen to information, students notice the process by which they accept, reject, and assess it. They write a brief essay analyzing their personal evaluation process.

4. Students select an occupation of interest and discuss in a brief essay the information skills that would be useful in that endeavor.

5. Students write a brief essay portraying the information society twenty-five to fifty years from now.

6. Students locate two editorials taking opposite sides of an issue. They analyze the two different points of view.

Notes and Suggested Reading

1. Peter Fenner and Martha C. Armstrong, *Research: A Practical Guide to Finding Information* (Los Altos, Calif.: Kaufman, 1981), p. 143.

2. Alvin Toffler, *The Third Wave* (New York: Bantam, 1980), pp. 349–351.

3. John Naisbett, *Megatrends: Ten New Directions Transforming Our Lives* (New York: Warner Books, 1982), p. 19.

4. Theodore Roszak, *The Cult of Information: The Folklore of Computers and the True Art of Thinking* (New York: Pantheon, 1986).

5. Fenner and Armstrong, *Research*, p. 143.

6. Harlan Cleveland, "Educating for the Information Society," *Change* 17:13–21 (July–Aug. 1985).

7. United Nations Educational, Scientific and Cultural Organization and the International Council of Scientific Unions, *UNISIST: Study Report on the Feasibility of a World Science Information System* (Paris: UNESCO, 1971), p. 11.

8. *Statistical Yearbook* (Paris: UNESCO, 1987), pp. 5–9. The actual figures are 2,608,100 international scientists and engineers in 1970; 3,236,900 in 1975; and 3,756,100 in 1980.

9. Naisbett, *Megatrends*, p. 24.

10. David S. Backer, "Prototype for the Electronic Book," in *Electronic Publishing Plus: Media for a Technological Future*, ed. Martin Greenberger (White Plains, N.Y.: Knowledge Industry, 1985), p. 131.

11. Blaise Cronin, "The Information Society," *Aslib Proceedings* 38:121–29 (Apr. 1986).

12. Daniel Bell, *The Coming of Post-Industrial Society: A Venture in Social Forecasting* (New York: Basic, 1973), p. 20.

13. Naisbett, *Megatrends*, p. 14.

14. Ibid., pp. 12, 21.

15. Elizabeth Frick, "Information Structure and Bibliographic Instruction," *The Journal of Academic Librarianship* 1:14 (Sept. 1975). These concepts are further developed in Elizabeth Frick, "Teaching Information Structure: Turning Dependent Researchers into Self-Teachers," in *Theories of Bibliographic Education: Designs for Teaching*, eds. Cerise Oberman and Katina Strauch (New York: Bowker, 1982), pp. 193–209.

16. The paradigm was originally published in Deborah Fink, "Concepts for Bibliographic Instruction in This Time of Transition," in *Energies for Transition: Proceedings of the Fourth National Conference of the Association of College and Research Libraries*, Baltimore, Maryland, April 9–12, 1986, ed. Danuta A. Nitecki (Chicago: American Library Assn./ACRL, 1986), pp. 49–51.

17. An analysis of this situation is offered in the introduction to *Field Guide to Alternative Media: A Directory to Reference and Selection Tools Useful in Accessing Small and Alternative*

Press Publications and Independently Produced Media, ed. Patricia J. Case (Chicago: Task Force on Alternatives in Print/Social Responsibilities Round Table/American Library Assn., 1984).

18. Frick, "Information Structure," p. 14.

19. Charles K. West, *The Social and Psychological Distortion of Information* (Chicago: Nelson-Hall, 1981), pp. 78, 80–81.

20. *Statistical Yearbook*, pp. 6–11, 6–13, 7–161.

21. U.S. Bureau of the Census, *Statistical Abstract of the United States: 1987*, 107th ed. (Washington, D.C.: Govt. Print. Off., 1986), p. 531.

22. Robert H. Ennis, "A Taxonomy of Critical Thinking Dispositions and Abilities," in *Teaching Thinking Skills: Theory and Practice*, eds. Joan Boykoff Baron and Robert J. Sternberg (New York: Freeman, 1987), pp. 9–26.

23. Barry K. Beyer, "Critical Thinking: What Is It?" *Social Education* 49:271 (Apr. 1985).

24. Mona McCormick, "Critical Thinking and Library Instruction," *RQ* 22:340 (Summer 1983).

25. Stephen D. Brookfield, *Developing Critical Thinkers: Challenging Adults to Explore Alternative Ways of Thinking and Acting* (San Francisco: Jossey-Bass, 1987), pp. x, 7–9, 44.

26. Ibid., p. 44.

27. See, for example, Richard W. Paul, "Critical Thinking and the Critical Person," in *Thinking: The Second International Conference*, eds. D. N. Perkins, Jack Lochhead, and John Bishop (Hillsdale, N.J.: Erlbaum, 1987), pp. 373–403; and Richard W. Paul, "Critical Thinking: Fundamental to Education and for a Free Society," *Educational Leadership* 42:4–14 (Sept. 1984).

28. Brookfield, *Developing Critical Thinking*, p. 76.

Chapter *2*

Reference Tools

A reference collection serves as a gateway to both the library's holdings and an array of information. Reference tools provide brief factual information, introductions to subjects, and access to sources of information. Researchers should know the many types of reference tools, how to become familiar with a tool, and how to assess reference works, as well as the organization of a reference collection.

Because of their function and centrality to the library, reference tools are commonly perceived as ultimate authorities. To the contrary, these works are as susceptible to the politics of development, publication, and dissemination as any other publications. Researchers should challenge, compare, and validate the information acquired from reference works.

Subsequent chapters focus on encyclopedias and dictionaries, card and online catalogs, and print and computer-based indexes; this chapter introduces a miscellany of additional tools to familiarize students with the diversity of reference collections and an approach to reference tools.

What Is a Reference Tool?

"Tools" is a particularly apt designation for items in a reference collection, because they have been brought together to answer questions and identify sources of information. Daniel Gore defines a reference book as:

> Any book not designed for consecutive or complete reading: it is
> a book to which you refer, usually very briefly, for a specific bit
> of information or a concise introduction to a topic, ignoring the

rest of its contents. For this reason, and because they are in heavy demand, reference books do not circulate. The arrangement of their contents is commonly either alphabetical or chronological (sometimes both), a circumstance that makes the location of particular facts quite simple, but consecutive reading nearly impossible. But since the internal arrangement of reference books does not follow any one fixed pattern . . . it is always prudent to read enough of their prefaces to learn, in each case, how the book is to be used.[1]

Three categories of reference tools can be identified: fact, finding, and hybrid. According to the authors of *Learning the Library*:

> Fact tools are those reference works that are consulted, usually briefly, with a specific simple, factual question in mind, the purpose of which is to yield a fairly discrete answer to such a specific question. . . . Finding tools do not give information directly, as do fact tools, but they lead the student/researcher to the information contained in another format.[2]

Hybrid tools are those that can serve both purposes.

There are many types of reference sources, including the well-known encyclopedias, dictionaries, periodical indexes, and catalogs. Additional sources include indexes to reviews, biographical information, and material in collections, as well as almanacs, directories, sources of statistics, atlases and gazetteers.

How to Study Reference Books

Many reference sources appear complex or baffling at first glance. Far too often, users overlook special features and fail to take full advantage of a source. Gore's advice to read enough of the preface to learn how to use a reference book merits following. Researchers can quickly and systematically overview a new reference book in order to determine its purpose, scope, arrangement, and type of entry, as well as how to use it most efficiently.

A concise and time-honored procedure for studying reference books was first set forth by Isadore Gilbert Mudge in an early edition of the ALA *Guide to Reference Books* and subsequently reprinted through the ninth edition. According to the procedures, the student should first examine the title page carefully for information about the scope of the work, the author, the publisher, and the imprint. Mudge advised next reading the preface or introduction for:

1. Further information as to scope of work
2. Special features claimed
3. Limitations, if any
4. Comparison with other books on same subject.

Then the book itself should be examined to note the arrangement, entries, cross-references, supplements, and indexes. Mudge elaborated:

> In examining both Preface and articles, note any evidence of lack of impartiality; e.g., if the book deals with a controversial subject, religious, political, etc., does it represent only one side; or, in the case of a biographical work, are the selection of names, kind and length of an article, etc., determined in any way by the desire to secure subscribers.

Finally, Mudge encouraged students to be aware of variations in alphabetical arrangements and to look for the extent of revisions in new editions.

How to Evaluate Reference Works

Beyond becoming familiar with a reference book, the researcher should also assess the work. A work can be evaluated in and of itself or in terms of its usefulness for a particular need. The distinction is significant. An excellent source may prove useless for a particular question, but that does not necessarily reduce its excellence, especially if the question is not within the scope of the work. On the other hand, a poorly edited and produced work may be the only source that satisfies a certain need, but that does not necessarily augment its general quality. This distinction should be reinforced, because students are inclined to undervalue those tools that fail to answer their immediate need and to disregard the potential of such sources for future uses.

The following outline is an overview of points that a reference source reviewer might take into consideration.

   I. Reference work in general
      A. Format and ease of use
         1. General appearance, size
         2. Binding, paper, type face, illustrations, page makeup, margins, etc.
         3. Pagination, running titles, textual divisions, etc.

B. Arrangement and access
   1. Alphabetical, chronological, topical
   2. Cross-references
   3. Table of contents, index
   4. Introduction, guide to user
C. Authority
   1. Reputation of publisher
   2. Qualifications of author, editor, compiler, contributors
   3. Sources of data
D. Aim and scope
   1. Purpose
   2. Intended use and users
   3. Thoroughness, completeness of entries
   4. Balance in selection and treatment
   5. Range, depth of coverage
E. Timeliness and accuracy
   1. Date of latest copyright
   2. Revision policy or supplements, yearbooks, etc.
   3. Currency of statistical data, illustrations, bibliographies, etc.
   4. Documentation
   5. Consistency
F. Treatment and style
   1. Point of view
   2. Language
   3. Quality, level of writing
   4. Facts vs. opinions
G. Special features
   1. Supplementary material (illustrations, glossary, appendix, etc.)
   2. Aids to users (dividers, color coding, etc.)
II. Reference work in relation to a particular need
   A. Ease of use
      1. Figuring it out: user guide, etc.
      2. Access: contents, index, arrangement, subject headings, etc.
      3. Convenience of arrangement: information concentrated or scattered
      4. Understandable data
   B. Coverage
      1. Relevance
      2. Thoroughness

　　　3. Completeness
　　　4. Timeliness
　C. Usefulness
　　　1. New material or new approach
　　　2. Appropriate level
　　　3. Additional references

　Students may also find it useful to compare the work to others of its type and to assess it overall. Additional sets of evaluative criteria are provided by Norman Stevens and Jovian Lang; Jean Key Gates and William Katz each offer criteria for each type of reference tool.[3] Students will find that most of these considerations are applicable to the assessment of information as well as reference sources.

A Miscellany of Reference Tools

Many types of sources comprise a library's reference collection in addition to the familiar encyclopedias and dictionaries, card or online catalog, and periodical indexes. Knowledge of the full array of reference tools enables researchers to identify sources for information that may not be readily available and to locate brief factual information. Subsequent units cover the fact and finding sources essential for most library research. As an introduction to the use and variety of reference works, a miscellany of additional sources, including examples of three types of finding tools and four types of fact tools, is presented here.[4]

INDEXES TO MATERIALS IN COLLECTIONS

Most card or online catalogs do not list the contents of books, but there are many special indexes that provide access to material in collections. In the following important titles, dates indicate the time period covered.

Essay and General Literature Index. 1900–　. New York: Wilson.
Granger's Index to Poetry. 1904–　. New York: Columbia Univ. Pr.
Play Index. 1949–　. New York: Wilson.
Short Story Index. 1953–　. New York: Wilson.
Speech Index. 1935–　. New York: Scarecrow.

INDEXES TO REVIEWS

Book reviews are useful for evaluating the quality and suitability of a book, biographical information that may be included, and plot digests. Theater and film reviews are useful for production information (dates, cast, etc.), assessing the quality of a production, and plot digests. Product reviews are useful for making consumer choices.

Book reviews often include something about the author, an overview and summary, a value judgment, and comparison to similar works. To locate a book review, students should know the author, title, and date of publication. There are a number of special indexes for identifying book reviews, including:

Book Review Digest. 1905–   . New York: Wilson. Covers more than eighty selected periodicals and includes quotations from the reviews listed. At least four fiction and two nonfiction reviews must appear in the indexed periodicals for a book's reviews to be included. Subject and title indexes.

Book Review Index. 1965–   . Detroit: Gale. Indexes nearly 400 periodicals. Includes citations to all reviews in journals covered. Coded for reference work, child, young adult, or periodical. Title index.

Index to Book Reviews in the Humanities. 1960–   . Williamston, Mich.: Thompson. Indexed by author of book only. Covers approximately 350 periodicals.

New York Times Book Review Index. 1896–1970. New York: New York Times. Separate volumes for author, title, byline, subject, category (i.e., genre).

There are also book review indexes covering specific disciplines (e.g., literature, drama, film, anthropology, history, sociology). In addition, most periodical and newspaper indexes include book reviews, which may be listed under the author of the reviewed book or in a separate review section in the back of the index volumes.

Theater and film reviews also may be identified by consulting newspaper and periodical indexes. It is useful to know the year of production or release as well as the title. The following sources provide the review itself:

New York Theater Critic's Reviews. 1940–   . New York: Critics' Theater Reviews. Publishes the complete reviews from eight New York publications and stations.

The New York Times Theater Reviews. 1870–   . New York: New York Times Book Co. A compilation of all theater reviews published by the newspaper, with indexes by person, title, and production company.

Landers Film Reviews: The Information Guide to 16mm Films and Multi-Media Materials. 1956– . Escondido, Calif.: Landers Associates. Arranged by title with a subject index, entries include a paragraph-length review.

The New York Times Film Reviews 1913–1968. 6 vols. New York: New York Times and Arno Press, 1970. The actual reviews from the newspaper are here reproduced. Includes title, person, and corporate indexes.

Variety Film Reviews. 1907– . New York: Garland. Chronologically arranged reproductions of *Variety* reviews. Title index included.

Product reviews can also be identified by consulting standard periodical and newspaper indexes. The following index is dedicated to such reviews:

Consumer's Index to Product Evaluations and Information Sources. 1973– Ann Arbor, Mich.: Pierian Press. Lists citations to reviews under sixteen categories, including health, home, office, education, and computing (covers hardware, software, and databases).

INDEXES TO BIOGRAPHICAL INFORMATION

Biographical information can be found in many places; encyclopedias, yearbooks, and directories are particularly useful. Periodical indexes can be searched for biographical information as well. There are also dictionaries and indexes devoted to information about people. "CT" is the Library of Congress class for general biographical tools. Biographical information on persons of a particular country can be located in the D, E, or F category for that country. Information on persons in a particular field will be in the Library of Congress class for that field. Subject headings useful for locating biographical dictionaries include:

BIOGRAPHY—DICTIONARIES
[COUNTRY]—BIOGRAPHY—DICTIONARIES
[FIELD OF ENDEAVOR]—BIOGRAPHY—DICTIONARIES
[CLASS OF PERSONS]—BIOGRAPHY—DICTIONARIES

The field (e.g., science) or the class (e.g., scientists) can also be subdivided by a geographical location.

Biographical dictionaries vary in coverage and format: they may be retrospective or current, general or special, essay or tabular. Retrospective dictionaries include individuals who were not alive at the time of publication, while current dictionaries include only those who were alive at the time of publication. General dictionaries cover all fields, while specialized biographical dictionaries are limited to a particular field. Entries may be in essay format or limited to a paragraph of basic facts (usually with many abbreviations).

When using biographical dictionaries, the introductory materials should be perused to learn which of the preceding apply. It is also important to note how biographees were selected and how the biographical information was obtained. As Eugene Sheehy points out:

> Unscrupulous publishers will sometimes include articles on comparatively unknown persons, with the expectation, or on condition, that these persons will pay for inclusion or will subscribe for the book. The inclusion of such articles puts the book in the commercial or "vanity" class and casts doubt upon the authority of all articles.[5]

Generally, it is best to begin a search for biographical information in specialized indexes, such as:

Biography and Genealogy Master Index. 1975–   . Detroit: Gale. Emphasizes living persons in the United States and Canada. Functions as an index to biographical dictionaries.

Biography Index. 1946–   . New York: Wilson. Covers periodicals, books of individual and collective biographies, and incidental biographical materials in books.

Index to Women of the World from Ancient to Modern Times: Biographies and Portraits. Norma Olin Ireland. Westwood, Mass.: Faxon, 1970. Analyzes 945 collective biographies; approximately 13,000 women are included.

Marquis Who's Who Publications: Index to All Books. 1974–   . Chicago: Marquis. Also includes *Who Was Who* volumes. Lists Marquis publications.

ALMANACS

Almanacs contain a wide variety of brief facts and statistics. Many contain directory and biographical information. Most will give a chronology of the major events of the preceding year.

Information Please Almanac Atlas and Yearbook. 1974–   . New York: Viking.

World Almanac and Book of Facts. 1868– . New York: Newspaper Enterprise Association, Inc.

DIRECTORIES

Directories include a variety of information about people and organizations, e.g., names, addresses, history, and publications.

Congressional Directory. 1809– . Washington, D.C.: Govt. Print. Off.
Congressional Staff Directory. 1859– . Mount Vernon, Va.: Congressional Staff Directory Ltd.
United States Government Manual. 1935– . Washington, D.C.: Govt. Print. Off.
Encyclopedia of Associations. 1956– . Detroit: Gale.
Research Centers Directory. 1960– . Detroit: Gale.
Polk's. . . City Directory. 1913– . Kansas City, Mo.: R. L. Polk.

Directories for a particular field, organization, and so forth can be located in a card or online catalog under the appropriate [SUBJECT HEADING]—DIRECTORIES, or by consulting:

The Directory of Directories: An Annotated Guide to Business and Industrial Directories, Professional and Scientific Rosters, and Other Lists and Guides of All Kinds. 1980– . Detroit: Information Enterprises. Distributed by Gale.

SOURCES OF STATISTICS

Statistics are available on many subjects. They can be found in almanacs and encyclopedias, as well as in special statistical compilations, such as those listed below.

Statistical Yearbook. 1949– . New York: United Nations.
Statistical Abstract of the United States. 1879– . Washington, D.C.: Govt. Print. Off.
Historical Statistics of the United States: Colonial Times to 1970. Washington, D.C.: Govt. Print. Off., 1975.
European Historical Statistics, 1750-1970. New York: Columbia Univ. Pr., 1975.
Countries of the World and Their Leaders Yearbook. 1974– . Detroit: Gale.
The Europa Yearbook: A World Survey. 1926– . London: Europa.
The Statesman's Yearbook: Statistical and Historical Annual of the States of the World. 1864– . New York: St. Martin's.

ATLASES AND GAZETTEERS

An atlas is a bound set of maps with an index (often called a gazetteer) and usually an accompanying text. Various kinds of thematic maps may be included that graphically display political, economic, statistical, and historical information. Most students will be quite familiar with this type of source, although they may not have thought of it as a reference tool. Students are not likely to know that a gazetteer can also be a separate publication that serves as a dictionary of place names, useful for identification, spelling, pronunciation, location, and other miscellaneous information.

The following provide information on identifying and assessing atlases:

Kister, Kenneth F. *Kister's Atlas Buying Guide: General English-Language World Atlases Available in North America.* Phoenix, Ariz.: Oryx, 1984.

"Atlases." In *Guide to Reference Books.* 10th ed. Eugene P. Sheehy, ed. Chicago: American Library Assn., 1986.

Subject Headings for Reference Tools

The *Library of Congress Subject Headings* provides a variety of form subdivisions for identifying reference works. A subject heading may be subdivided by any of the following:

ABSTRACTS
ATLASES
BIBLIOGRAPHY (further
    subdivided into CATALOGS
    and UNION LISTS)
BIO-BIBLIOGRAPHY
BIOGRAPHY
BOOK REVIEWS
CATALOGS
CHRONOLOGY
DICTIONARIES
DICTIONARIES AND
    ENCYCLOPEDIAS

DIGESTS
DIRECTORIES
GUIDE-BOOKS
HANDBOOKS, MANUALS, ETC.
HISTORY
INDEXES
MAPS
OUTLINES, SYLLABI, ETC.
STATISTICS
YEARBOOKS

Sample Learning Objectives

Concepts to understand:

The nature and types of reference sources.
The functions and some titles of each of the following:
  Indexes to material in collections
  Indexes to reviews
  Indexes to biographical information
  Almanacs
  Directories
  Statistical sources
  Atlases and gazetteers.

Skills to apply:

Familiarizing oneself with a reference source.
Assessing a reference source.

Sample Discussion Questions

1. What is a reference source?
2. What are some types of reference sources?
3. What reference sources might be labeled "finding"?
4. What reference tools might be labeled "factual"?
5. What are some "hybrid" reference works?
6. Why should you take time to familiarize yourself with a new reference source? How can you do so quickly and efficiently?
7. Why should you assess reference sources? What are some points to consider?
8. How can you identify smaller units within books, such as poems, plays, essays?
9. What might reviews be used for? How can they be identified?
10. What is the difference between biography and bibliography?
11. Other than in direct research on an individual, why might a researcher seek biographical information?
12. What are some sources that include biographical information?
13. What is the best way to begin seeking biographical information?
14. What kinds of information are included in an almanac?

15. What federal publications are useful for directory and statistical information?
16. What kinds of information do atlases provide?
17. What is a gazetteer?

Sample In-Class Activities

1. As a class, tour the reference department.
2. Students each have a different reference work before them. They examine the title pages and share comments as a class about what is observed. They peruse the preface or introduction and share comments again. The entire book is overviewed to discuss observations. Finally, evidence of impartiality or bias is sought and discussed.
3. In small groups, students familiarize themselves with a reference work according to the guidelines in "How to Study Reference Books" in this chapter.
4. In small groups, students assess a reference work according to the outline on "How to Evaluate Reference Works" in this chapter.
5. Small groups each work with a different type of reference work (e.g., index to material in collections, review index, biographical index, almanac, directory, statistical source, atlas, or gazetteer). Group members study an example of a source in the category to determine its purpose, scope, arrangement, and type of entries. They develop three questions that can be answered by the source. To the class at large, a spokesperson briefly describes the source, reads the questions, and indicates how the questions are indicative of the purpose of the source.

Sample Take-Home Exercises

1. Students create a map of the reference department.
2. Students choose a source from each of five different types of miscellaneous sources (a total of five sources). They study each source to determine its purpose, scope, arrangement, and entries. They list three "real life" questions that they actually use the source to answer, and include the answers. They state how those questions are indicative of the nature of the source.

3. Students choose two different sources in any one category of miscellaneous sources (e.g., the *World* and *Information Please* almanacs), and compare their coverage for several different appropriate questions.
4. Students select one of the miscellaneous sources and evaluate it in general or in relation to a topic.

Notes and Suggested Reading

1. Daniel Gore, *Bibliography for Beginners*, 2nd ed. (New York: Appleton, 1973), p. 91.

2. Anne K. Beaubien, Sharon A. Hogan, and Mary W. George, *Learning the Library: Concepts and Methods for Effective Bibliographic Instruction* (New York: Bowker, 1982), pp. 83–84.

3. Norman Stevens, "Evaluating Reference Books in Theory and Practice," in *The Publishing and Review of Reference Sources*, eds. Bill Katz and Robin Kinder. *The Reference Librarian*, number 15, Fall 1986 (New York: Haworth, 1987), pp. 13–15. Jovian Lang, "Evaluation of Reference Sources Published or to Be Published," in the same issue of *The Reference Librarian*, pp. 58–62.

See also chapters covering particular types of reference tools in Jean Key Gates, *A Guide to the Use of Books and Libraries*, 5th ed. (New York: McGraw-Hill, 1983) and William A. Katz, *Introduction to Reference Work, Volume I: Basic Information Sources*, 4th ed. (New York: McGraw-Hill, 1982).

4. For alternative selections, see Gates, *A Guide to the Use of Books and Libraries*, and Katz, *Introduction to Reference Work*.

5. Eugene P. Sheehy, ed., *Guide to Reference Books*, 10th ed. (Chicago: American Library Assn., 1986), p. 279.

Chapter 3

Research and the Disciplines

Research is the application of a systematic procedure for the accretion of understanding or knowledge. The universe of knowledge is typically approached through the academic disciplines of the sciences, social sciences, and humanities. The discipline through which a researcher approaches a topic provides both a literature and a context, perspective, vocabulary, and methodology. The more students know about the disciplines that cover a subject, the more they will know about what kind of information is available and how it can be accessed. They should also be aware of the political nature of the disciplines and the value of interdisciplinary approaches.

Research and the Scientific Method

Research is both a means to an end, i.e., the location of specific, finite information and a form of inquiry, i.e., the seeking of understanding to increase knowledge. Research is a systematic process for recognizing a need for data, acquiring and validating that data, and deriving conclusions from them. Types of data include experimental, mathematical, social, historical, and bibliographical. Techniques of validation are typically determined by the methodology of the researcher's discipline or, for the nonspecialist, are based on critical thinking skills. Pure (or original or primary) research is the discovery of new knowledge, and scholarly (or bibliographic or secondary) research is the synthesis and interpretation of existing knowledge.

The scientific method is one example of a systematic procedure for research. It is a controlled investigation following an organized process that is repeatable and stresses doubts. The scientific method includes the following steps:

44

1. Statement of problem
2. Collection of data
3. Formation of hypothesis
4. Testing of hypothesis
5. Rejection or nonrejection of hypothesis
6. Communication of results.

This approach is commonly construed as rational, neutral, and objective. Contemporary analysis, however, reveals the intrinsic nature of subjectivity in all examination and inquiry. Since Michael Polanyi's in-depth critique of the objective-subjective polarity and advocacy of "personal knowledge" rather than scientific detachment, both scientists and social scientists have acknowledged and begun to explore the role of subjectivity in research.[1] At an annual conference, anthropologists discussed subjectivity in ethnography; the traditional "participant-observer" methodology was challenged as artificial, biased, and intrusive.[2] Parker Palmer seeks a "spirituality of education" by rejecting both objectivity and subjectivity in favor of truth through relationship or community.[3] Gary Zukav describes the revelations of contemporary physics:

> According to quantum mechanics there is no such thing as objectivity. We cannot eliminate ourselves from the picture. We are a part of nature, and when we study nature there is no way around the fact that nature is studying itself. . . . Scientists, using the "in-here—out-there" distinction, have discovered that the . . . distinction may not exist! What is "out there" apparently depends, in a rigorous mathematical sense as well as a philosophical one, upon what we decide "in here."[4]

A research strategy is the library equivalent of the scientific method, and bibliographic research is also influenced by external forces. In this chapter, the disciplinary structure is considered; in a later chapter, critical evaluation is explored as a check for both external and internal biases.

The Disciplines

The knowable universe is so vast, so intricate, that understanding is sought and organized according to areas of knowledge, or disciplines. As diagramed in figure 7, the disciplines serve to organize knowledge and to provide perspectives and methodologies for exploring the knowable universe. The literature of a discipline is the mechanism by which knowledge is recorded and disseminated, providing communication among practitioners and disciplines. Libraries, especially academic libraries, collect, preserve, and provide access to the literatures of the disciplines. Library researchers explore those literatures for learning and perhaps generate a written report. Published reports add to the literature of the discipline and enhance the world of knowledge.

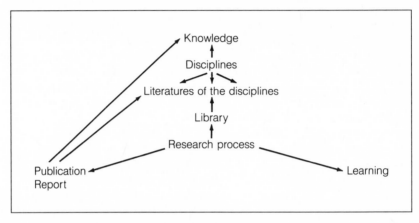

Figure 7. Research in context

A familiar model of the disciplines is the university structure. Academic departments are the institutionalized manifestations of the disciplines, promoting research, teaching, and service. Introductory courses in each department acquaint undergraduate students with the structure, vocabulary, methodology, and key contributors of the field; graduate courses and research and teaching assistantships train future practitioners. Faculty members are considered the experts of the field: they study the existing knowledge base and add to the literature and knowledge of the field.

Dimensions and Development of a Discipline

Michael Keresztesi defines the disciplines as "knowledge producing and disseminating systems" and explores the interrelations between research and bibliography. He identifies four dimensions of a discipline: epistemological, sociological, historical, and bibliographical.[5]

The epistemological dimension is the structure, content, and methodology of the discipline. Dressel and Marcus note five components of a discipline's structure: the subject matter and concepts; the linguistic symbols (verbal, numerical, or nondiscursive); the method of inquiry; the values (including attitudes, ethics, and esthetics); and the field's relation to other disciplines.[6]

The sociological dimension of a discipline includes its internal organization and social status and support. Most disciplines maintain a professional structure through associations and standards. The disciplines are institutionalized through academia, institutes, or the government. In fact, Keresztesi claims that "there is no bona fide scientific or scholarly discipline in the United States today outside the university."[7] The status of a discipline is evidenced monetarily by funding and salaries, socially by its academic or professional place, and epistemologically by the control and use of its research.

The historical background of a field, especially key contributors and classic texts, is often relevant to research. The current developmental stage or maturity of a discipline is also of interest. Keresztesi identifies three stages in the growth of a field and the types of literature that characterize each stage.

In the early pioneering stage, practitioners and their communication comprise an "invisible college" with no formal structure or literature. The early adherents may be followers of an innovator or a core of experimenters branching off from an established field. Written records may be only personal correspondence, typescripts, in-house reports, minutes, or informal proceedings. It is difficult to obtain access to such a network without a personal contact. The subsequent elaboration and proliferation stage produces a growing body of publications and secondary access sources that are collected and made available by libraries. The establishment stage marks the academic integration of a discipline and the availability of standardized sources, such as encyclopedias, subject dictionaries, textbooks, handbooks, annual reviews, etc.

The bibliographic or documentation dimension of a discipline is obviously of concern to researchers. Communication among practitioners will include journals, proceedings, annual reviews, and monographs. The distribution and significance of each of these modes will vary from field to field, as will the length of time required for publication and the importance of currency. The researcher will need to know not only what is available, i.e., the information sources or the information structure; but also how it is accessed, i.e., the reference sources or the bibliographic structure.

To recap, the library researcher might ask the following questions about a discipline:

What is the historical background of the field and its current developmental stage?
What are the broad subject areas covered by the field?
What is the social and economic status of the discipline?
How do practitioners work?
Where do practitioners work?
How are practitioners organized?
How do practitioners communicate?
How is the literature of the discipline accessed?

To answer these questions, students can consult a basic textbook for the field or a general encyclopedia article on the discipline. Another direct and expedient approach is to peruse a bibliographic guidebook to determine the access structure of a discipline or an abstracting index to discover subjects of current interest. The tables of contents in such sources reveal much about the field in the areas they cover.

Comparing the Disciplines

Disciplines are commonly grouped into the humanities, sciences, and social sciences. Their methods of inquiry can be characterized accordingly as interpretive, experimental, and a combination of those approaches. Fields within each discipline area are considerably divergent and may overlap categories: history is variously included as a humanity or a social science, and psychology may be claimed by both science and the social sciences. Nevertheless, within each area there are enough fundamental similarities in methodology, focus, and use of the literature to make generalizations useful for library research.[8]

The humanities scholar typically works alone among a variety of bibliographic text sources, including original and unpublished materials, in libraries and special collections. This scholar focuses on both recent and enduring monographs, but also looks to journal literature for critical analysis over time. Knowledge in the humanities is not built cumulatively on a body of facts and theories, but rather on individual analysis and interpretation of creative and intellectual constructs to discover relationships and assess value. It is a highly personal form of knowing, based on a close examination—as intuitive as systematic—of symbolic products.

The scientist is often engaged in pure research, which may be a team effort. Particulars of the natural world are examined, often in a laboratory, for regularities, patterns, and relationships in order to establish general theories. Knowledge in the sciences is cumulative, and theories provide a context for experimentation. Books and periodicals are primarily archival; scientists may consult current journal articles, but they rely on paper presentations, direct communication with colleagues, and, increasingly, electronic transmission of information. Methodological validity and individual detachment are stressed.

The social scientist collects, studies, and applies social data, often collaboratively. The fields of the social sciences are comparatively recent, and the methodologies vacillate between quantitative and qualitative. Knowledge in these fields is not generally cumulative and tends to be interdisciplinary, based on primary data generated by and about people, but not necessarily by social scientists. The diverse literature, growing exponentially, is both monographic and serial, and it is used by practitioners as well as by academics. The social scientist may have a scattered approach to published sources and rely on colleagues and citations, rather than indexes, for access.

Evaluating the Disciplinary Structure

Although the disciplines are central to the ways we "know" the universe and organize that knowledge, they are, nevertheless, artificial and political. According to the physicist Fritjoff Capra, "Quantum theory . . . reveals an essential interconnectedness of the universe. It shows that we cannot decompose the world into independently existing smaller units."[9] Fragmentation and overspecialization are hazardous when experts fail to honor the fact that no form of inquiry is isolated; it relates to and affects the whole. Contemporary interests and concerns, particularly ecological and international, underline the importance of interdisciplinary approaches. Palmer sees "promising movements towards community in the world of intellect today" in such emergent epistemologies as feminist thought, Black and Native American scholarship, and the new physics.[10]

The disciplinary structure is also suspect because of political forces that impose priorities. The sciences are more highly and consistently subsidized by the government than the humanities and social sciences. The sciences are also better supported by universities because of their grant-winning potential. Once a discipline reaches the establishment stage, a topical or methodological hierarchy will emerge. Practitioners who are out of the mainstream or are especially innovative may find it difficult to get published in the more prestigious journals or proceedings. Pressures within individual campuses or departments, including the publish or perish syndrome, influence what is researched and disseminated. Areas of study go in and out of favor. Citation indexing and evaluation based upon that technique encourage researchers to cite themselves and colleagues. The scholarly and scientific community thus becomes a self-perpetuating and self-limiting structure, as Kenneth Boulding notes:

> Science...buys its success at a price; indeed at a high price. The price is a severe limitation of its field of inquiry and a value-system which is as ruthless in its own way in the censoring of messages as the value system of primitive man. Messages which will not conform to the subculture are condemned as illusion. Furthermore, the world of the scientist is the world of the repeatable, the world of the probable. The rare occurrence, the nonrepeatable event, the unanswerable question elude him.[11]

Most student research topics can be approached from several different disciplines. Generally, in the process of focusing a topic for research, one disciplinary approach will appear more useful than others. While student researchers will find that knowledge of the disciplinary structure and a particular relevant discipline will enhance their research, they can achieve even greater breadth and depth of understanding by viewing their topic from a variety of perspectives.

Sample Learning Objectives

Concepts to understand:

Research as a method of inquiry.
The disciplines as an approach to the knowable universe.
The development of a disciplinary literature and access sources.
Characteristics of the sciences, humanities, and social sciences.
The political nature of the disciplines.
The value of interdisciplinary approaches.

Skills to apply:

Answering basic questions about a discipline.
Applying knowledge of a discipline to research.

Viewing a topic from a broader perspective than a single discipline.

Sample Class Discussion Questions

1. What is research?
2. What are the value and shortcoming of the scientific method?
3. Is objectivity possible?
4. What are the disciplines and what are their functions?
5. How does the discipline with which you approach a topic affect your research?
6. How is knowledge of a discipline useful in library research?
7. What do you need to know about a discipline?
8. What do you need to know about the literature of a discipline?
9. For students majoring in a science: how would you characterize research in the sciences?
10. For students majoring in a humanity: how would you characterize research in the humanities?
11. For students majoring in a social science: how would you characterize research in the social sciences?
12. What are some of the conceptual and methodological problems created by the disciplinary division of the universe and knowledge?
13. Why do you think the sciences are better supported by the government and academia than the other disciplinary areas?
14. Contrast the perspectives of specialized and interdisciplinary study.

Sample In-Class Activities

1. Arrange a disciplines panel. Invite library or faculty representatives of the three discipline areas (sciences, social sciences, humanities) to discuss the nature of research in their area. Encourage interaction among the panelists as well as between the students and panelists.
2. As a class, students choose a topic and determine the disciplines from which it might be approached. They discuss the difference in perspective of each discipline. They list other disciplines that are less obviously related to the topic, and, by forcing relationships, establish even more perspectives on the topic.

Sample Take-Home Exercises

1. In a brief essay, students develop a portrait of a discipline by answering the following questions:
    What are the historical background of the field and its current developmental stage?
    What are the broad subject areas covered by the field?
    What is the social and economic status of the discipline?
    How do practitioners work?
    Where do practitioners work?
    How are practitioners organized?
    How do practitioners communicate?
    How is the literature of the discipline accessed?
2. In a brief essay, students discuss how the research on a given topic would be shaped by the discipline from which it was approached.

Notes and Suggested Reading

1. Michael Polanyi, *Personal Knowledge* (Chicago: Univ. of Chicago Pr., 1958).

2. Ellen K. Coughlin, "Anthropologists Explore the Possibilities, and Question the Limits, of Experimentation in Ethnographic Writing and Research," *Chronicle of Higher Education* 30: A5+ (Nov. 1988).

3. Parker J. Palmer, *To Know as We Are Known: A Spirituality of Education* (San Francisco: Harper, 1983).

4. Gary Zukav, *The Dancing Wu Li Masters* (New York: Bantam, 1979), pp. 31, 92.

5. Michael Keresztesi, "The Science of Bibliography: Theoretical Implications for Bibliographic Instruction," in *Theories of Bibliographic Education*, eds. Cerise Oberman and Katina Strauch (New York: Bowker, 1982), pp. 1–26.

6. Paul L. Dressel and Dora Marcus, *On Teaching and Learning in College: Reemphasizing the Roles of Learners and the Disciplines* (San Francisco: Jossey-Bass, 1982), pp. 89–99.

7. Keresztesi, "The Science of Bibliography," p. 8.

8. For more in-depth discussions, see Topsy N. Smalley and Stephen H. Plum, "Teaching Library Researching in the Humanities and Sciences: A Contextual Approach," in *Theories of Bibliographic Education: Designs for Teaching*, eds. Cerise Oberman and Katina Strauch (New York: Bowker, 1982), pp. 135–170; Ron Blazek and Elizabeth Aversa, *The Humanities: A Selective Guide to Information Sources*, 3rd ed. (Englewood, Colo.: Libraries Unlimited, 1988), pp. 1–9; and William Webb et al., *Sources of Information in the Social Sciences: A Guide to the Literature*, 3rd ed. (Chicago: American Library Assn., 1986), pp. 3–12.

9. Fritjoff Capra, *The Tao of Physics: An Exploration of the Parallel between Modern Physics and Eastern Mysticism*, 2nd ed., rev. and updated (Boston: Shambhala, 1985), p. 137.

10. Parker J. Palmer, "Community, Conflict, and Ways of Knowing," *Change* 19:24 (Sept.–Oct. 1987).

11. Kenneth E. Boulding, *The Image: Knowledge in Life and Society* (Ann Arbor, Mich.: Univ. of Michigan Pr., 1961), p. 71.

Chapter 4

Encyclopedias and
Dictionaries

Since most undergraduate researchers are seeking information in subject areas they have not previously explored, they will usually do well to begin with an overview of the subject. Books, periodical articles, or news digests may serve this purpose, but general and subject encyclopedias are readily available and easily used, and their raison d'etre is to provide background information.

Most students are aware of the value of dictionaries for writing a report, but few will turn to specialized word books as part of the research process. Even experienced researchers can usually improve their search strategy by consulting dictionaries to develop a vocabulary control list.

Because students will already be familiar with encyclopedias and dictionaries, the emphasis here is on the usefulness of these tools in the early stages of the search process and their roles in the determination and perpetuation of knowledge. From this latter perspective, the importance of critical evaluation is underlined. Students should also be alerted to the increasing availability of encyclopedias and dictionaries online and on CD-ROM.

General and Subject Encyclopedias

General encyclopedias contain informational articles of varying length on subjects in all fields of knowledge. Subject encyclopedias contain articles of greater depth and detail on topics within the particular subject area. Many subject encyclopedias are called "dictionaries," but a true subject dictionary provides brief, concise definitions for specialized terms in the subject area, while a subject encyclopedia provides longer, more in-depth articles.

Students may have been instructed not to use encyclopedias for research. As a principal source of information, encyclopedias are inappropriate for research; however, for the descriptive exploration of a subject, they are very useful and acceptable for several reasons. Encyclopedias are particularly useful for an introduction to a subject: articles typically include background information, an overview of concepts, and definitions of key terms. Illustrations often provide additional clarification. An encyclopedia index is an excellent place to begin developing a vocabulary control list; additional terms may be suggested by the article itself. The organizational structure of an encyclopedia article may suggest an approach to the topic, or the student may discover an issue of particular interest. Many articles will include a bibliography, which can lead to further sources of information.

The alphabetical arrangement of most encyclopedias belies the actual complexity of their organization. Many subjects will not be covered in a separate entry, but will be imbedded in a broader or related article. Special sections or features may be included in addition to the alphabetical listing of articles. Students must be encouraged to follow the procedural guidelines for "How to Study Reference Books" in chapter 2. They should always examine the organization, consult the index, and follow through on cross-references. The organization of the fifteenth edition of the *Britannica*, for example, is likely to seem baffling at a first glance; careful study of the arrangement is required to take full advantage of this set. Students should also be advised to consult encyclopedia yearbooks.

While most students will be familiar with general encyclopedias, few will be aware of one-volume and subject encyclopedias. Single-volume encyclopedias may be useful for brief factual information. Subject encyclopedias focus on a particular discipline or subject area and are therefore more detailed and technical than general encyclopedias. This generalization will not always hold true, however, especially when a subject encyclopedia is less current than a general encyclopedia, and most subject encyclopedias are not updated with great frequency.

Comparisons among encyclopedias and between general and subject encyclopedias can be very revealing. Despite the fact that most encyclopedia articles are written or at least reviewed by subject specialists, discrepancies do occur among, and even within, encyclopedias. Controversial topics or aspects of subjects are often glossed over or neglected. Bias may be perceived not only in the treatment of controversial topics, but also in which topics are included and excluded and the weight assigned to subjects by the extent of coverage. Given the information explosion and changing social mores and attitudes, accuracy and acceptability are complex variables.

Encyclopedias are generally perceived as neutral and authoritative, when, in fact, like any form of communication, they are the products of individuals communicating from their own frames of reference and unique sets of biases. Encyclopedias reflect their time and place no less than other sources of information. The danger of misrepresentation by them is compounded by their very purpose of simplifying and reducing information. And the danger in the fact of their misrepresentation is that they serve to record and are therefore seen to legitimatize the consensus of what constitutes knowledge in our society.

Language and Subject Dictionaries

Most undergraduates will be quite familiar with language dictionaries; in fact, they are the source most likely to be available in the home or dorm room. Nevertheless, many users fail to take full advantage of the wide range of special features often included in dictionaries, especially the unabridged variety, such as maps, full-color plates, guides to style and form, specialized listings, etc. Furthermore, dictionaries are useful for more than checking spelling and definitions. As Sheehy notes:

> Theoretically the dictionary is concerned only with the word, not with the thing represented by the word, differing in this respect from the encyclopedia which gives information primarily about the thing. Practically, however, the large modern dictionary is very often encyclopedic and gives information about the thing as well as the word, thus combining the features of the two types of reference books.[1]

Language dictionaries include most or all of the following: spelling, syllabication, pronunciation, etymology, meaning, synonyms, antonyms, word forms, syntax, usage, quotations, abbreviations, slang, foreign terms and phrases, new words, biographical and geographical information, tables, signs, symbols, illustrations, and other supplementary material.

Language dictionaries are useful in research for defining a topic and key terms; identifying synonyms as suggestions for subject headings; locating brief information on people, places, and things; and assisting in the communication of research results in clear and correct written form. They may be particularly useful as a part of descriptive exploration to determine the precise meaning of key terms and to discover shades of meaning or usage that may shed new light on the topic. Authors and speakers often begin the explication of a topic with a dictionary definition and etymology. The origins and changing meaning of a word may reveal much about subtle social attitudes and shifts. The way a word has been used in quotations can also deepen understanding.

Dictionaries may be unabridged (i.e., over 250,000 entries) or desk or college (i.e., 130,000–180,000 entries).[2] The latter type includes juvenile dictionaries. Another distinction concerns usage designations. Some dictionaries, notably the second edition of *Webster's*, are prescriptive, indicating how language *should* be used. Since the third edition of *Webster's*, however, most dictionaries have been descriptive, recording how language *is* used. Proponents of the former approach wish to maintain standards, while those who favor the latter approach view language as a dynamic reflection of changing culture.[3]

Another controversy centers on the inclusion of curse words and terms of sexual or racial denigration. Although the trend is toward increasing inclusion, objections to the availability of dictionaries which include such terms are sometimes manifested in attempts to remove "permissive" dictionaries from school libraries. Even the most descriptive of dictionaries will label derogatory terms as "vulgar," "offensive," or "contemptuous." However, as Katz notes, variations and inconsistencies in the assignment of these designations have provoked charges of sexism and racism.[4] He also documents studies that show that more positive attributes are assigned to male-associated words than to female-associated words.[5]

As encyclopedias legitimatize the social knowledge base, dictionaries legitimatize language itself, which is never static.[6] Etymologies trace the dynamic nature of vocabulary; the increasing number of entries in unabridged dictionaries and the publication of dictionary supplements also demonstrate the growth of language. The efforts of women and other minorities to achieve equity have been directed towards changing language as well as society, because words are the building blocks of thoughts, attitudes, and social norms. New words and new connotations, often spawned by science and technology as well as social developments, must pass tests of time and appearances in print, however, before they are sanctioned by dictionary publishers.[7]

In addition to English language, other language, and bilingual (such as Spanish-English and English-Spanish) dictionaries, a variety of word books are available, including listings of slang, dialect, etymology, synonyms and antonyms, usage, abbreviations and acronyms, rhyming words, suffixes and prefixes, new words, and specialized terms. Subject dictionaries define terms within the context of a particular discipline or subject area. The definitions tend to be rather technical. Subject dictionaries and encyclopedias represent the standardization and codification of a discipline's knowledge base. In terms of the evolution of a field, the availability of dictionaries and encyclopedias generally indicates that a discipline has become established.

Locating and Evaluating Encyclopedias and Dictionaries

General encyclopedias are located in the Library of Congress "A" classification; English language dictionaries are shelved under "PE." Subject encyclopedias and dictionaries are shelved in the LC class covering the particular subject area. There are four ways to identify a subject encyclopedia or dictionary for a topic: (1) by browsing in a reference department under the LC class for that topic; (2) by looking in a catalog under the [TOPIC]—DICTIONARIES (or —DICTIONARIES AND ENCYCLOPEDIAS); (3) by consulting a bibliographic guide; and (4) by consulting *First Stop: The Master Index to Subject Encyclopedias* (Phoenix, Ariz.: Oryx, 1988), which includes subject dictionaries as well as encyclopedias.

The procedures described in chapter 2 for "How to Study Reference Books" and "The Evaluation of Reference Works" are directly and appropriately applied to encyclopedias and dictionaries. In addition, guidelines developed specifically for evaluating these sources are provided by Sheehy, Katz, and Kister.[8]

Sample Learning Objectives

Concepts to understand:

Applications of encyclopedias and dictionaries in research.
The difference between general and subject encyclopedias.
Why it is important to use the encyclopedia index.
What may be included in a dictionary.
The variety of word books.
How encyclopedias and dictionaries may be biased.

Skills to apply:

Identifying and locating general and subject encyclopedias and dictionaries.
Evaluating dictionaries and encyclopedias.
Citing entries in encyclopedias and dictionaries.

Sample Class Discussion Questions

1. What is the purpose of an encyclopedia?
2. What encyclopedia are you most familiar with? How have you typically approached it?
3. Why is it important to consult encyclopedia indexes?
4. To what extent are encyclopedias unbiased, authoritative sources of information?
5. What dictionary do you have at home? What special features does it have?
6. Do you think children should have access to dictionaries which include curse words and terms of racial or sexual denigration?
7. Should dictionaries maintain the standards of a language or simply report words as they are used?
8. Should language be changed to reflect the concerns of particular populations within a culture?
9. What is a thesaurus?

Sample In-Class Activities

1. Given a particular topic, students go to the reference department to identify and locate a subject encyclopedia and subject dictionary relevant to the topic. Students look up and cite an entry in each source related to the topic.
2. Working in small groups, students study and describe a word book (other than a language dictionary). Each group reports their findings to the class at large.
3. In small groups, students develop three to five questions they would like to have answered about a given topic.[9]

Example:

Topic: Vitamins

What is the recommended daily requirement of the major vitamins for children, adults, and the elderly?
Are vitamin supplements necessary, and if so, when?
What is the current thought on megavitamin therapy?
Does increased vitamin intake help or hinder a weight loss program?
What are the symptoms of vitamin deficiency?

Looking for their topic in a general and subject encyclopedia, students compare the coverage of their topic and evaluate each encyclopedia. (See chapter 2, "Reference Tools," for guidelines on "How to Study Reference Books" and "How to Evaluate Reference Works.") Each group reports its findings to the class at large. Sample topics and subject encyclopedias:

Civil War—*Encyclopedia of Black America*
Schizophrenia—*Encyclopedia of Psychology*
Consumer price index—*Encyclopedia of Economics*
Pre-Raphaelite art movement—*Encyclopedia of World Art*
Suicide—*Encyclopedia of Bioethics*
Kabuki theater—*McGraw-Hill Encyclopedia of World Drama*
Satan—*Encyclopedia of Religion*
Epidemiology—*Encyclopedia of Aging*

4. Working in small groups, students identify key terms for a given topic using a general dictionary, a thesaurus, and a subject dictionary to develop a vocabulary control list consisting of synonymous, related, broader, and narrower terms. Maximum of five terms in each list.

Example:

Topic: Diets and Dieting

Synonyms:	Weight loss	Related	Exercise and diet
	Weight loss	terms:	Fasting
	programs		Calories
	Reducing		Obesity
	Caloric counting		Diet therapy
Broader	Nutrition	Narrower	Low-fat diet
terms:	Appetite	terms:	Starch blockers
	Cooking		Cambridge diet
	Health		Macrobiotic diet
	Food habits		Vegetarianism

Sample topics and subject dictionaries:

Ragtime music—*Harvard Dictionary of Music*
Taxation—*Dictionary of Economics and Business*
Metaphysics—*Dictionary of Philosophy*
Racism—*Dictionary of Anthropology*
Epistemology—*Penguin Dictionary of Sociology*
Oligopoly—*American Political Dictionary*
Deterrence—*World Encyclopedia of Peace*
Midwife—*Feminist Dictionary*

Sample Take-Home Exercise

This exercise is based on the students' use and evaluation of background sources.

PART 1: ENCYCLOPEDIAS

1. Locate a background article on a subject in a general or subject encyclopedia or both. Supply the encyclopedia title and the publication year (be sure to use the most recent year available).
2. If you cannot find an article on your specific topic, look for background on a broader subject area. List the words you looked under in the encyclopedia index to find information on your subject. List all the terms you tried, whether they worked or not, and mark the ones that were useful with an asterisk.
3. Note all explanatory material included in the encyclopedia. If you find any of the following, briefly note its value:

   Preface or introduction
   Guide to use
   List of contributors
   List of abbreviations
   Other features.

4. Photocopy both sides of the title page of the encyclopedia and photocopy your article. Bring the photocopies to the next class period. Briefly summarize the article and note its usefulness for your subject.

PART 2: IN-CLASS DISCUSSION

1. Could you identify a subject encyclopedia? How would you expect general and subject encyclopedias to differ? If you looked at both, did you in fact find a difference?
2. Why is it important to use the index?
3. What did you learn from the index and the article itself about the vocabulary associated with your subject?
4. Did you have to go to an even broader subject area to find a relevant article?
5. What kind of information did you get from the article?
6. What does the organizational structure of the article suggest to you?
7. Did you detect any bias in the treatment of your subject?
8. Do citations, statistics, etc., in the article reflect the currency of the publication year?
9. What did this article contribute to your understanding of the subject?
10. Who authored the article?
11. Did the article include a list of additional sources?
12. What can you learn about the encyclopedia itself from the title page?
13. What did the explanatory material contribute to your use and understanding of the encyclopedia?
14. How easy was it to find information on your subject:
    Were the subject headings appropriate and useful?
    Was the information in one or two articles or scattered?
    Did the encyclopedia refer you to related information?
    Was the organization of the encyclopedia straightforward?
15. What did you observe about the layout, use of illustrations, etc.?

PART 3: DICTIONARIES

1. Use a general language dictionary, a thesaurus, and a subject dictionary, if available (consult with the instructor or a reference librarian), to begin developing a vocabulary control list for your topic. List the title and publication year for each dictionary consulted.
2. Develop a set of terms that you can look under for information on your topic, following the example on page 59.

3. Cite one encyclopedia article and one dictionary entry.

4. In a brief essay, evaluate in general (not in relation to your topic) one of the encyclopedias or dictionaries you consulted. (See the section in chapter 2 on "How to Study Reference Books" and "The Evaluation of Reference Works.") You may wish to compare the source to some of the others you used.

Notes and Suggested Reading

1. Eugene P. Sheehy, ed., *Guide to Reference Books*, 10th ed. (Chicago: American Library Assn., 1986), p. 146.

2. William A. Katz, *Introduction to Reference Work. Volume I: Basic Information Sources*, 2nd ed. (New York: McGraw-Hill, 1974), p. 252.

3. Ibid. Also see William A. Katz, *Introduction to Reference Work*, 4th ed. (New York: McGraw-Hill, 1982).

4. Katz, *Introduction to Reference Work*, 4th ed., p. 304.

5. Katz, *Introduction to Reference Work*, 2nd ed., p. 250.

6. An extensive catalog of types of changes in the English language is presented in Thomas J. Creswell and Virginia McDavid, "Usage: Change and Variation," in *The Random House Dictionary of the English Language*, 2nd ed. unabr. (New York: Random, 1987).

7. "The Recent Growth of English Vocabulary," in *9,000 Words: A Supplement to Webster's Third New International Dictionary* (Springfield, Mass.: Merriam, 1983), pp. 13a–17a.

8. "Encyclopedias" and "Language Dictionaries," in Sheehy, *Guide to Reference Books*; "Encyclopedias: General and Subject" and "Dictionaries" in Katz, *Introduction to Reference Work*, 4th ed.; Kenneth F. Kister, *Encyclopedia Buying Guide: A Consumer Guide to General Encyclopedias in Print*, 3rd ed. (New York: Bowker, 1981); Kenneth F. Kister, *Dictionary Buying Guide: A Consumer Guide to General English-Language Wordbooks in Print* (New York: Bowker, 1977).

9. Susan Anthes participated in the development of this and the following activity.

Chapter 5

Creative Problem Solving

Library research is a lengthy, complex, and varied process that requires a variety of skills. In addition to the skills traditionally identified with using the library, students can draw upon other techniques to enhance the process. At various points, the researcher will need to generate ideas or tactics for selecting a topic, for identifying a new approach for data collection, or for communicating the final results. Creative problem solving provides fresh perspectives for alleviating some common difficulties in library research.

In chapter 1, critical thinking was defined both as an attitude (a willingness to examine closely one's own as well as other points of view) and as an approach to information that draws upon the skills of critical evaluation and creative problem solving. Creative problem solving was defined as the ability to make judicial choices by working integratively from a multiplicity of imaginatively generated alternatives. Students can develop their imaginative and judicial thinking skills by applying creative problem-solving techniques to stimulate the generation of ideas and to identify criteria for making choices.

What Is Creativity?

Creativity has been explored in terms of personal attributes, the creative product, the creative process, and factors that may foster or inhibit creativity.[1] Discussions in the literature commonly focus on lists of traits or conditions that foster creativity. For example, Sidney Parnes identifies the following qualities inherent in the creative individual: fluency, flexibility, originality, elaboration, sensitivity, and evaluative ability.[2]

Drawing upon a variety of theoretical bases, the authors of *Dimensions of Thinking* articulate five aspects of creativity:

1. Creativity takes place in conjunction with intense desire and preparation.
2. Creativity involves working at the edge rather than the center of one's capacity.
3. Creativity requires an internal rather than an external locus of evaluation.
4. Creativity involves reframing ideas.
5. Creativity can sometimes be facilitated by getting away from intensive engagement for awhile to permit free-flowing thought.[3]

The creative result may be a work of art or practical application. There is some disagreement in the literature as to whether a product should be deemed creative if it is just new to its creator but not entirely new.[4] Some writers further postulate that the creative product must demonstrate both uniqueness and value.[5]

The moment of creative insight is a highly personal experience that has been described by authors, artists, inventors, and scientists. Bob Samples offers this description:

> When the inventive mode is functioning, a total synergic kind of knowing evolves. Exploration has the quality of a dream. Objects, processes, and conditions emerge, merge, and dissolve with no reason. The configurations that last do so because they have personal meaning, but not necessarily a public reason. Great courage is required at this stage because ego is transcended. Psychological fragilities are forgotten and they impose no retarding influence on the freedom of exploration. The total energies of intellectuality, emotionality, and sexuality merge into a force at once passive and aggressive. There is resolution to be, but not to control. The euphoria of discovery provides a continuing, peaceful orgasm of pan-existence. Giving and taking, dismissing and possessing all become the same. In this state of viable openness the invention, the creation, the peak experience ...happens."[6]

In contrast to the supreme thrill of creative illumination, the process required to achieve that moment is at times slow, laborious, and agonizing—at the very least, hard work requiring dedication and perseverance. Despite individual resistance to this process and adverse social conditioning, creativity is among the attributes generally associated with a fully developed or actualized individual.

Although creativity is an inherent human characteristic, it is typically inhibited by social, educational, and employment structures. James Adams identifies various blocks to creativity, including conceptual, perceptual, cultural, environmental, emotional, intellectual, and expressive blocks.[7] In essence, blocks may be internal or external. Internal blocks include faulty apprehension or articulation of a problem, as well as inadequate skills for solving a problem. Emotional blocks may also hinder creativity, especially self-disparagement and fear. External blocks include distractions in the environment, lack of support, and social attitudes that devalue the creative process.

Although most individuals are limited by belief structures that stifle natural creativity, simple techniques can stimulate the imagination. Given the culturally determined sanctions against creativity, most students will benefit from the application of such techniques to research.

Creative Problem Solving

According to Parnes, "When a person makes creative decisions...he first speculates on what 'might be' from a variety of viewpoints; then he senses and anticipates all conceivable consequences or repercussions of the variety of actions he has contemplated; finally he chooses and develops his best alternatives—in full awareness."[8]

For any given problem, there will be not only a variety of solutions, but also alternative methods for arriving at a solution. The first and most difficult step is the choice to commit oneself to solving the problem and selecting a method. The rest is procedural.

Creative problem solving is defined here as the structured alternation between creative (or right brain) and judicial (or left brain) thinking. The creative problem solver defers judgment by consciously separating creative from judicial thinking at various stages of the creative problem-solving process.

Explications of right and left thinking modes are plentiful in the popular literature. Particularly useful and graphic charts are provided by both Betty Edwards and Gabriele Lusser Rico.[9] The left mode is logical, rational, and linear, while the right mode is intuitive, imagistic, and holistic. Left brain thinking may be characterized as rule-bound and critical; right brain thinking as unbounded and creative.

Whether this division is scientifically accurate or not, it is a useful metaphor for the primary processes in problem solving and research: generating ideas or hypotheses, and selecting or testing them. Creativity is often stifled by an internal judge, which frequently censors ideas before they are fully articulated, dismissing them as stupid, ridiculous, or impossible. The very act of expressing ideas, however, can often lead to additional ideas or refinements. Therefore, the goal in creative problem solving is to ignore the internal censor initially and generate as many ideas as possible. Only after all thoughts have been expressed is the judge called upon to rationally develop and apply criteria for selection. Thus both the left and right modes are appropriate and valuable depending on the desired results; the goal is to be able to freely invoke either mode as appropriate.

In *Applied Imagination*, a seminal work on creativity, Alex Osborn identifies three stages in the creative problem-solving process: fact-finding, which includes problem definition and data gathering and analysis; idea-finding, including idea production and development; and solution-finding, which includes evaluation and adoption. His description of the problem-solving sequence is illustrative of the alternation between modes:

1. Think up all phases of the problem. . . .
2. Select the sub-problems to be attacked. . . .
3. Think up what data might help. . . .
4. Select the most likely sources of data. . . .
5. Dream up all possible ideas as keys to the problem. . . .
6. Select the ideas most likely to lead to solution. . . .
7. Think up all possible ways to test. . . .
8. Select the soundest ways to test. . . .
9. Imagine all possible contingencies. . . .
10. Decide on the final answer. . . .[10]

These steps are roughly parallel to the research process. Steps 1 and 2 represent problem formulation; steps 3 and 4 are equivalent to developing a search strategy; steps 5 and 6 are similar to data collection; steps 7 and 8 represent evaluation; and steps 9 and 10 are equivalent to the organization and communication of results. Various techniques can be applied at each step to structure the alternation, including brainstorming, making lists and forcing relationships, and visual representation.

BRAINSTORMING

Brainstorming was developed in the late 1930s by Osborn as an approach to generating ideas in company conferences. He discovered that ideas, when readily articulated without the threat of evaluation by group members, inevitably stimulate more ideas by associative thought. By the 1950s, Osborn lamented that the idea had become "too popular too fast, with the result that it was frequently misused."[11]

Viewed as a tool and not a cure, and properly applied, however, brainstorming is a powerful mechanism for individual as well as group fluency. Osborn's rules specify that:

1. *Criticism is ruled out.* Adverse judgment of ideas must be withheld until later.

2. *Free-wheeling is welcomed.* The wilder the idea, the better; it is easier to tame down than to think up.
3. *Quantity is wanted.* The greater the number of ideas, the more the likelihood of useful ideas.
4. *Combination and improvement are sought.* In addition to contributing ideas of their own, participants should suggest how ideas of others can be turned into *better* ideas; or how two or more ideas can be joined into still another idea.[12]

Brainstorming has obvious application to the generation of subjects or aspects of a subject for a research topic. It is also useful for creating a list of alternatives at any point in the research process where the student feels stuck. In fact, listmaking is an effective structure for individual brainstorming. Students may find informal listmaking in notebooks, journals, and so on useful for approaching a variety of problems, as well as for stimulating creativity.

LISTMAKING

A structured form of listmaking is attribute listing, which was developed by Robert Crawford and is described by both Osborn and John Arnold.[13] In this approach, all of the characteristics of an object or idea are listed and then changed or combined to suggest new aspects. Features may be structural or conceptual. Usually it is most effective to categorize the properties, creating several lists that may be manipulated horizontally as well as vertically. This technique is applied to problem formulation in chapter 7.

Combining features or ideas in new or unexpected ways is called forcing relationships.[14] Using attribute or other lists, the creative problem solver associates one idea with another, allowing the results to suggest new ideas. The simile and metaphor are examples of imaginative literary associations.

VISUAL REPRESENTATION

Recent interest in the dual hemispheres of the brain has produced a proliferation of methods for structuring alternation between the left and right modes. Techniques of visual representation to generate ideas and conceptualize thoughts are particularly useful for the research process, and students are likely to find them as useful for taking notes during lectures, most writing, and general problem solving.

Tony Buzan describes the goal of "mindmapping" as "to recall everything your mind thinks of around the central idea."[15] A mindmap on creative problem solving appears in figure 8; notice:

Words are printed and underlined.
All lines are connected.
Some concepts are connected with arrows.
Broader categories are boxed.
Points are developed from broader to narrower.

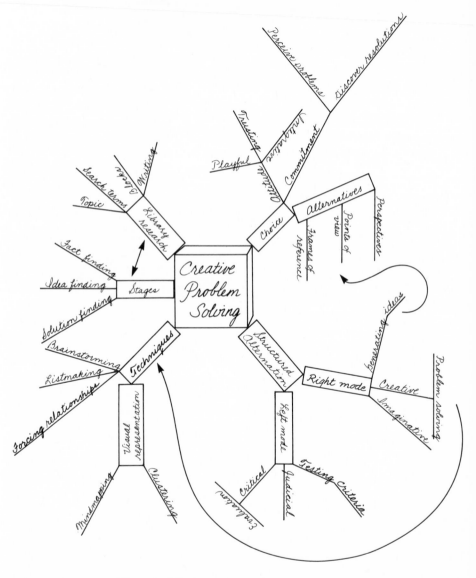

Figure 8. Mindmap of creative problem solving

"Clustering" is a similar technique described by Rico:

> To create a cluster, you begin with a nucleus word, circled, on a fresh page. Now you simply let go and begin to flow with any current of connections that come into your head. Write these down rapidly, each in its own circle, radiating outward from the center in any direction they want to go. Connect each new word or phrase with a line to the preceding circle. When something new and different strikes you, begin again at the central nucleus and radiate outward until those associations are exhausted.[16]

Attitudinal Aspects of Creative Problem Solving

In addition to brainstorming and visual representation, an open, integrative attitude is required for creative problem solving. First, the student must be willing to perceive problems and to view problem solving as the discovery of inherent resolutions. Problem-solving techniques are most effectively applied as games for the right brain; one's imagination resists coercion but delights in play.

Another aspect is trusting the process. One reward of applied problem solving is the ability to deliberately alternate modes. There is also an enhanced awareness of the automatic shifts that signal the inherent power of the mind. The practiced problem solver enjoys initiating the process and trusting that it will complete its course. Often, just the suggestion of a problem will be enough to set the imagination in motion: encouraged to seek resolution and left alone to incubate thoughts, the right brain will usually offer results at an unexpected moment.

Finally, the student should seek integration, i.e., a melding of all that has been set in motion, including the problem, alternative solutions, selection criteria, and one's complete self, to shape a new whole. The complexities of information and libraries in the learning society necessitate the application to research of such dynamic skills and results. Students are likely to discover that these are life-enhancing as well as research-enhancing experiences.

Sample Learning Objectives

Concepts to understand:

The nature of creativity.
Inhibitions to creativity.

The nature and value of creative problem solving.
The role of creative problem solving in library research.

Skills to apply:

Brainstorming.
Making lists and forcing relationships.
Mindmapping.
Clustering.

Sample Class Discussion Questions

1. What is creativity?
2. What qualities do you associate with a creative person?
3. Is creativity inherent or developed?
4. What is the value of creativity?
5. How is a creative product developed?
6. What inhibits your own creativity?
7. How does our culture discourage creativity?
8. What stimulates your creativity?
9. What might parents, teachers, and employers do to foster creativity?
10. What characterizes the right and left modes of thinking?
11. What is creative problem solving?
12. How do you typically approach problems?
13. What techniques are you aware of for solving problems?
14. What kinds of problems are you likely to encounter in library research?
15. What applications to research do you see for brainstorming, listmaking, and visual representation?
16. What other applications for these techniques can you see?

Sample In-Class Activities

1. The guidelines for brainstorming are presented to the class. As a class or in small groups, students brainstorm for solutions to a problem (examples follow). Students develop a set of criteria for selecting a solution and select a solution based on those criteria.

How can libraries be made easier for untrained users?
What skills for students in the information society should be required for graduation from college?
How can parking problems on campus be alleviated?
How can recycling on campus or in the community be improved?
What are some alternatives to grading in college?

2. Individually, in small groups, or as a class, students develop several metaphors for the library or college or the information society by listing attributes and forcing relationships.
3. Individually, students develop a mindmap or cluster on the information society or library research or a topic of choice.

Sample Take-Home Exercises

1. Students select something of concern in their own lives to develop a solution for. They choose one or more creative problem-solving techniques to apply to the issue. In two weeks, they report back (without providing personal details) as to whether the situation has changed.
2. Students use brainstorming to generate a list of at least twelve possible research topics for this class. They develop a set of criteria for selecting a topic and select a topic based on those criteria. Students also use clustering or mindmapping to recall what they already know about the subject and to begin considering some aspects of the subject they may wish to pursue. They develop two more clusters or mindmaps to identify their own and social biases towards the selected topic.

Notes and Suggested Reading

1. Byron G. Massialas and Jack Zevin, *Creative Encounters in the Classroom: Teaching and Learning through Discovery* (New York: Wiley, 1968), pp. 11–16.

2. Sidney J. Parnes, *Creative Behavior Guidebook* (New York: Scribner, 1967), pp. 28–29.

3. Robert J. Marzano et al., *Dimensions of Thinking: A Framework for Curriculum and Instruction* (Alexandria, Va.: Association for Supervision and Curriculum Development, 1988), pp. 24–28.

4. Massialas and Zeven, *Creative Encounters in the Classroom*, p. 12.

5. Parnes, *Creative Behavior Guidebook*, p. 6.

6. Bob Samples, *The Metaphoric Mind: A Celebration of Creative Consciousness* (Reading, Mass.: Addison-Wesley, 1976), p. 100.

7. James Adams, *Conceptual Blockbusting: A Guide to Better Ideas* (San Francisco: Freeman, 1974).

8. Parnes, *Creative Behavior Guidebook*, p. 6.

9. Betty Edwards, *Drawing on the Right Side of the Brain* (Boston: Houghton, 1979); Gabriele Lusser Rico, *Writing the Natural Way: Using Right-Brain Techniques to Release Your Expressive Power* (Los Angeles: Tarcher, 1983).

10. Alex Osborn, *Applied Imagination: Principles and Procedures of Creative Problem-Solving*, 3rd ed. rev. (New York: Scribner, 1963), pp. 111, 207–209.

11. Ibid., p. 152.

12. Ibid., p. 156.

13. Ibid., pp. 175–176; John Arnold, "Useful Creative Techniques," in *A Source Book for Creative Thinking*, eds. Sidney J. Parnes and Harold F. Harding (New York: Scribner, 1962), pp. 253–254.

14. Parnes, *Creative Behavior Guidebook*, p. 159.

15. Tony Buzan, *Use Both Sides of Your Brain* (New York: Dutton, 1974), p. 90.

16. Rico, *Writing the Natural Way*, p. 35.

Chapter 6

Search Strategy

All too often, students find information in libraries through serendipity. They enter the library in a state of fear or dread and go to either the first source they encounter, which is likely to be a card or online catalog, or the source with which they are the most familiar, perhaps the *Readers' Guide*. Because they have given no consideration to the types of information they require, or access sources or search terms, the discovery of relevant sources is probably a "happy accident."[1]

A more effective approach to library use is a search strategy. When students begin by clarifying their need, considering possibilities, and deliberately organizing their search, they are more likely to identify the most useful materials. A search strategy can also be used to establish a balanced approach to a topic by anticipating political effects throughout the process. The goal, however, is not to preclude serendipity, which is often an important element in research, but to structure all possibilities, planned and accidental, with a dynamic interplay between critical evaluation and creative problem solving. In fact, the definition of serendipity includes sagacity as well as chance.

This chapter overviews the research process in order to present the steps that are included in a search strategy and to suggest tactics for an efficient, effective search. This course is structured to model a generalized research strategy; most of the steps in the strategy are covered separately in subsequent chapters. The objective of this chapter is not to enable students to develop their own strategy: that is an intended outcome of the complete course. The objective here is to acquaint stu-

---

This section uses the concepts in the author's article, "BI Line: A Column on Bibliographic Instruction: Enhancing the Search Strategy Model," *Colorado Libraries* 12:24–25 (Sept. 1986).

dents with an organizational approach to the entire research process, so that they will recognize each step as it is covered in the course and understand how it fits into the complete process. In subsequent chapters, then, students will learn each part of the research process, so that, upon completion of the course, they can systematically put together the parts to develop and implement their own search strategy.

The Search Strategy Model

A model can be defined as "a systematic description in graphic form of the main elements of any structure or process and of the relationships among these elements."[2] A search strategy model can be used to introduce the types of sources a "typical" researcher would consult in the order they are likely to be approached. The most common model, which appears frequently in both in-house instructional materials and in the literature of bibliographic instruction, lists the reference sources for accessing background information, books, periodical articles, and additional information.[3]

The search strategy model is useful because it organizes the potentially overwhelming array of reference tools into a systematic, problem-solving procedure for gathering information. The ideal result is for students to be able to remember the series of steps. Each step will suggest specific sources, or at least a type of source, that will provide access to a desired format of information.

A drawback to the presentation of a single, "correct" model, however, is that it may be narrowly perceived as the only approach to library research. In the attempt to simplify the process, it is also limited and constrained. A strategy that encourages a systematic, organized, and thorough search for most undergraduate topics may not be appropriate for some information needs, and it does not represent the approach of more experienced researchers.

Although the search strategy model as an organizational framework for library instruction is a time-proven method, the value of this approach can be enhanced by introducing alternative models to reinforce the potential for flexibility and variations on the model. The model in figure 9 is based on the ubiquitous model of unknown origins. Two alternative models demonstrate variations based on the researcher's topic and background. The model in figure 10 illustrates a permutation of the basic model when retrospective materials will not be available or useful for current interest topics.[4]

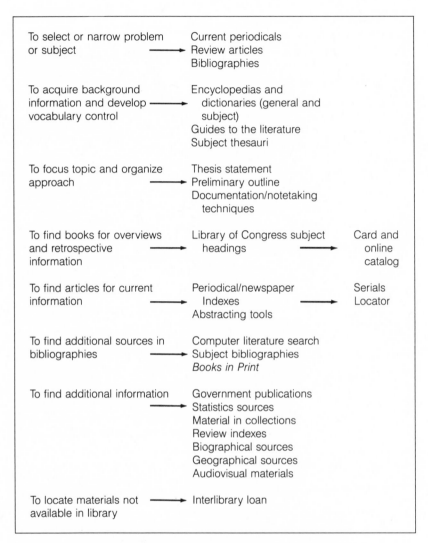

To select or narrow problem or subject	⟶	Current periodicals Review articles Bibliographies
To acquire background information and develop vocabulary control	⟶	Encyclopedias and dictionaries (general and subject) Guides to the literature Subject thesauri
To focus topic and organize approach	⟶	Thesis statement Preliminary outline Documentation/notetaking techniques
To find books for overviews and retrospective information	⟶	Library of Congress subject headings ⟶ Card and online catalog
To find articles for current information	⟶	Periodical/newspaper Indexes Abstracting tools ⟶ Serials Locator
To find additional sources in bibliographies	⟶	Computer literature search Subject bibliographies *Books in Print*
To find additional information	⟶	Government publications Statistics sources Material in collections Review indexes Biographical sources Geographical sources Audiovisual materials
To locate materials not available in library	⟶	Interlibrary loan

Figure 9. Basic search strategy model for undergraduates

A third model, in figure 11, illustrates the technique that researchers with background in the subject area can use to cycle backwards into the literature by following through on references in publications. The core bibliography developed in this fashion is then updated by

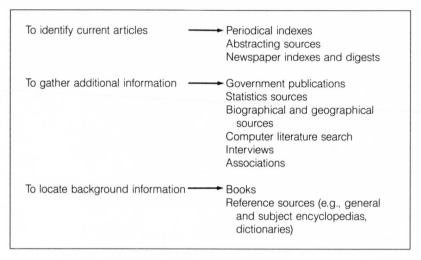

To identify current articles   ━━━━▶ Periodical indexes
                                                  Abstracting sources
                                                  Newspaper indexes and digests

To gather additional information   ━━━━▶ Government publications
                                                  Statistics sources
                                                  Biographical and geographical
                                                       sources
                                                  Computer literature search
                                                  Interviews
                                                  Associations

To locate background information ━━━━▶ Books
                                                  Reference sources (e.g., general
                                                  and subject encyclopedias,
                                                  dictionaries)

Figure 10. Search strategy model for current interest topics

consulting printed and online indexes, in particular the citation indexes, that enable the researcher to track publications of known authors.

Search Strategy Worksheet

Another presentation for the library search strategy is a worksheet, which offers both a visual representation of the process and an opportunity for students to develop a personalized plan for their topic. An example is provided in figure 12.

Search Tactics

While a research strategy is an overall plan of action, search tactics are discrete operations to further the search at specific points within it.[5] Tactics are useful to guide the research and to reduce the potential for information overload.

SELECTING AND FOCUSING A TOPIC

A topic may have been suggested by a personal need or been assigned; otherwise, the first step is to select a topic. Students often feel overwhelmed at this initial step; just knowing that library resources can be

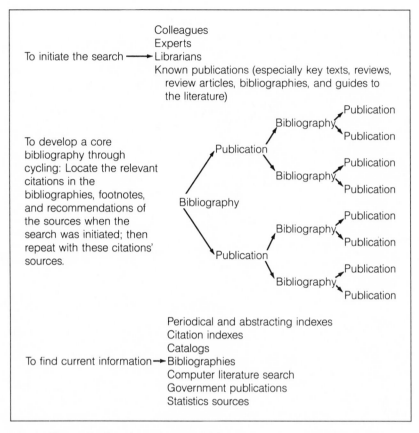

Figure 11. Search strategy model for researchers with background
in the subject area

applied at this step may be an important tactic. Potential researchers can peruse current periodicals to identify subjects of interest, browse through bibliographic series, such as the *Reader's Advisory Service*, the *Planning Librarian's Bibliographies*, or *Library of Congress Tracer Bulletins*. When the project is discipline-based, annual review sources may be consulted, such as *The Annual Review of Anthropology* or *Communication Yearbook*.[6]

Even when a topic has been assigned, students typically need assistance to narrow it to a workable size. Jon Lindgren suggests a useful tactic for shaping a topic by identifying a significant dispute on the subject from which to develop an argument or thesis. He provides a comprehensive listing of overview sources that can lead students to the evidence of disputed questions.[7]

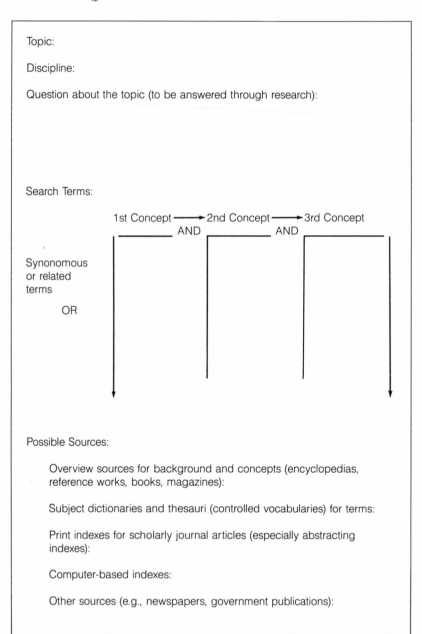

Topic:

Discipline:

Question about the topic (to be answered through research):

Search Terms:

1st Concept ──▶ 2nd Concept ──▶ 3rd Concept
_____ AND _____ AND _____

Synonomous
or related
terms

       OR

Possible Sources:

Overview sources for background and concepts (encyclopedias, reference works, books, magazines):

Subject dictionaries and thesauri (controlled vocabularies) for terms:

Print indexes for scholarly journal articles (especially abstracting indexes):

Computer-based indexes:

Other sources (e.g., newspapers, government publications):

Figure 12. Sample search strategy worksheet

DESCRIPTIVE EXPLORATION

Before beginning the actual data collection, the researcher should engage in a descriptive exploration or front-end analysis to become familiar with the subject area, establish search terms, initiate a preliminary bibliography, and determine organizational techniques. Since students may have little or no previous experience with a research topic, they should begin by answering some preliminary questions about the subject, including:

What disciplines would be likely to study this subject?
What is the historical development of the topic?
What are the key concepts and terms?
What are some "disputed questions" concerning this subject?
Who are some key thinkers and researchers in this area?
What are some of the key publications in this area?

Such questions can usually be answered with general and subject encyclopedias, subject dictionaries, and bibliographic guides.

Next, the student should determine what types of information are necessary to proceed. Considerations include general characteristics: factual or conceptual, concise or in-depth, popular or scholarly, current or retrospective, and primary or secondary. Format is another consideration: nonprint, book, periodical, newspaper, and grey literature.

Most of these terms will be clear to students, but some may require explanation. Popular materials are intended for a general audience, and the style and reading level will reflect a wide range of skills and interests. The authors of popular sources are typically professional writers and journalists who are unlikely to be experts on the subjects they address. Scholarly sources are intended for a particular field and will reflect the vocabulary and methodology of that field. The authors are generally experts in the field communicating with other experts. An expert can be defined as one who is well grounded in the literature of a discipline and advances the knowledge of that discipline. (This distinction is further elaborated in chapter 12.)

Primary sources are firsthand accounts and original works, including works of art, fiction, and philosophy, as well as letters, diaries, manuscripts, historical documents, laboratory and field reports, surveys, and interviews. Secondary sources are once-removed or secondhand reports, often based on primary sources. They include art reviews, literary criticism, editorials, and most journal articles; they provide analysis, interpretation, evaluation.

Grey literature is a diverse category of commercially unpublished and therefore fugitive or ephemeral materials, which often have immediate and practical applications but are difficult to identify and locate. Often, they are also difficult to store and preserve.[8] This category includes: theses and dissertations, in-house publications, pamphlets, working papers, conference papers and proceedings, preprints and offprints, unpublished reports, technical reports, surveys, and interviews. Much of the contemporary grey literature is available from organizations. Students should be encouraged to use sources beyond the library. Research can often be enhanced by visiting relevant organizations, interviewing individuals, or seeking primary material at events or in the media.

Once information needs have been established, a useful tactic is to predetermine the suitability of the topic in terms of the available library resources. A quick check of the library's catalog and one or two of the key indexes for the subject will reveal the extent and level of available information. Researchers can decide if enough material appears to be on hand and if that material is appropriate to their background. Should an overabundance of sources be discovered, students will know that the subject must be focused more narrowly and tactics for avoiding information overload must be applied.[9] This quick overview, then, not only eliminates a false start, it also provides a preview of the search, aiding in preliminary planning and organizational decisions.

During this descriptive exploration, the researcher should begin a vocabulary control list—a list of words, phrases, and subject headings with which to search for information on the topic. It may be useful to consult the *Library of Congress Subject Headings* at this point. The list should be developed throughout the search so that the researcher has an ongoing record of the terms that were useful and not useful, the sources they appeared in, and when they were used. This tactic is important because headings vary not only from source to source, but also from year to year within particular sources. (For more information on vocabulary control, see chapter 8.)

The front-end analysis includes planning and organizational determinations. Having established the types of information needed, the student can list the reference sources that provide access to that information, placing them in priority order. This prioritized list of access sources is generally perceived as the search strategy in library research.

USING BIBLIOGRAPHIC GUIDES
TO IDENTIFY ACCESS SOURCES

Bibliographic guides, sometimes called guidebooks or guides to the literature, are useful to survey and select access sources for a subject. These tools generally list reference sources by type (encyclopedias, indexes, etc.) and usually include annotations. There are two types of bibliographic guides: general and subject.

General guides to reference sources cover many disciplines or subject areas. They typically provide a classified listing of general reference tools useful in these fields and the major sources of particular fields, including subject guides to the literature. Subject guides to the literature, sometimes termed handbooks, checklists, or just bibliographies, are more detailed than general guides and are likely to provide discussions of the field and the resources. They may include an overview of the field, terminology, major reference sources (including bibliographies), indexes, journals, and lists of associations, as well as references to specific texts or articles.

The most used general guide is *Guide to Reference Books*, published by the American Library Association. There are also general guides for the social sciences, sciences, and humanities.[10] A wide variety of subject guidebooks is available and can be identified by consulting a general guide or the catalog under the subject heading BIBLIOGRAPHY—BIBLIOGRAPHY—[TOPIC]. The most current guidebooks can be identified with *American Reference Books Annual*.[11]

TIMELINE

The complete research process includes steps that precede and follow the search for information. A timeline is an effective approach for structuring the entire process. Most students conceptualize the research process as quickly gathering information and then writing the report. Typically, they not only neglect front-end analysis, but they also fail to allow sufficient time for identifying and locating material, evaluating sources, taking notes, responding to information gathered, filling in gaps, and writing multiple drafts. A timeline serves as a reminder of all the steps necessary for effective research. While original time estimates for each step are unlikely to be maintained, choices and adjustments can be exercised with forethought when the entire process has been laid out as a schedule.

A useful timeline includes the following steps with time estimates or entered on a calendar:

1. Select general subject, clarify requirements.
2. Engage in descriptive exploration and front-end analysis:
    a. Read background information.
    b. Determine a research question.
    c. Initiate vocabulary control list.
    d. Analyze information needs.
    e. Check suitability of topic.
    f. List and prioritize access sources and create timeline.
    g. Develop a preliminary outline.
3. Collect data.
    a. Identify materials using access sources.
    b. Locate materials.
    c. Read and evaluate materials, take notes, and document sources.
4. Assimilate and apply data.
    a. Respond to information gathered.
    b. Develop a thesis.
    c. Fill in gaps.
    d. Develop final outline.
    e. Draft, revise, edit, and proofread report.

RESEARCH QUESTION AND PRELIMINARY OUTLINE

During the course of the descriptive exploration, the researcher should pose a question about the topic as a focus for the search. At the outset of research, most students will not know enough about the topic to make a significant claim or take a stand, as required for a thesis statement. A research question (for example, "Are there circumstances that predispose individuals to abuse their children?" Or, "What are the environmental effects of tropical deforestation?") is a useful tactic for fostering a more open attitude. The researcher is then inclined to seek answers rather than information that corroborates a preconceived point of view. As a result of the research process, students discover the range of perspectives and critically evaluate this information to arrive at their own conclusions and formulate a final thesis, which will ultimately be expressed as a clear, pithy assertion.

The research question and a preliminary outline serve as criteria of selection; the final thesis and outline structure the communication of the search results. A preliminary outline is an important tactic for reducing information overload. Confronted with masses of information, the student uses the research question and outline to select the most relevant material based on focused information needs. Finally, techniques for note taking and documentation are also determined during front-end analysis. A subsequent chapter covers all of these organizational techniques.

DATA COLLECTION

The second major component of the research process is the actual data collection. Working from the prioritized list of access sources, the researcher identifies and locates books, periodical articles, and other information sources. One tactic for reducing the amount of time spent consulting access sources is to take advantage of the footnotes and bibliographies included in information sources as well as separately published subject bibliographies. Card and online catalogs are primarily locating tools that show the holdings of a particular library, while indexes (and trade bibliographies) are identifying tools that show what has been published on a given subject. Subject bibliographies and lists of sources consulted, however, have been selected by someone who is familiar with the subject.

A tactic for extending the search and inviting serendipity is browsing. Browsing is made possible by the classified arrangement of library materials. Because related materials are shelved together, the researcher can either determine the class or call number range for a subject and browse in those areas of the reference collection and the stacks, or, when seeking a particular item on the shelves, the researcher can browse around the item, looking for other relevant materials. Of course, all the materials will never be on the shelves at any one time; nevertheless, researchers will often discover through browsing items that were not identified even with a thorough and systematic search. Browsing is also possible in card and online catalogs.

Throughout the search process, researchers must remain alert to political influences. Recalling the cycle of information processing, researchers can anticipate potential limitations to the availability of and access to sensitive information, alternative materials, or multiple perspectives. These difficulties are highlighted throughout this course. Researchers must also monitor their own expectations and unconscious filtering of material that is contrary to their perspective. A deliberate effort is required to seek all sides. Critical evaluation is necessary to determine to what extent available materials actually represent the whole picture; creative problem solving is required to structure a well-balanced search and to go beyond what may be readily available.

Sample Learning Objectives

Concepts to understand:

The organization of this course as a generalized search strategy.
The functions of a search strategy and search tactics.
Using the library to select and focus a subject.
The purposes of descriptive exploration or front-end analysis.
Determining information needs.
Definitions of popular, scholarly, primary, secondary, and grey literature.
The importance of a vocabulary control list.
Organizing research with a prioritized list of access sources and a timeline.
The value of bibliographic guides.
The functions of a research question and outline.
The value of footnotes and bibliographies for research.
The potential of browsing.

Skills to apply:

Selecting a search strategy model to match information needs.
Posing basic questions about an unfamiliar research subject.
Identifying reference sources for a given subject.

Sample Class Discussion Questions

1. How could you select a topic for research?
2. How do you typically begin library research?
3. How can you focus a research subject?
4. What are some basic questions you might ask about a subject before beginning research?
5. How could you quickly answer those questions?
6. What are the formats of information?
7. What are the differences between, and some examples of, factual and conceptual information? Concise and in-depth? Popular and scholarly? Current and retrospective? Primary and secondary?
8. How can you determine whether a particular library's resources will be sufficient for researching a particular topic?

9. How can you determine what reference sources are available for a subject?
10. How are footnotes and bibliographies in publications useful in the research process?
11. How can you ensure a well-balanced search?

Sample In-Class Activities

1. In small groups, students develop models for library research as they typically conduct it and as they would ideally conduct it.
2. In small groups, students list the steps they would include in a research timeline.
3. In small groups, students pose preliminary questions about a given research topic and use encyclopedias to answer the questions.
4. In small groups, students are given copies of general and subject guidebooks. They compare the coverage for a given topic and report back to the class at large.
5. In small groups, students are given a topic and general and subject guidebooks. They develop a list of potentially useful reference sources for the topic.

Sample Take-Home Exercises

BIBLIOGRAPHIC GUIDES

Students explore general guidebooks relevant to a topic (Sheehy; Webb, Hurt, or Blazek and Aversa; and *American Reference Books Annual*) and respond to the following questions:

1. All disciplines: Sheehy. Scan the table of contents.
   a. In what section(s) and subdivision(s) is your topic covered?
   b. Under which heading(s) is your topic listed in the index? Do not confuse subject and title entries in the index. What additional sections or subdivisions (if any) did you discover?
   c. List some titles that sound useful, or state why you think Sheehy was not helpful for your topic.
   d. Comment on the value of this source to your research.

2. Answer the following questions for only one of these disciplines: social sciences (read chapter 1 of Webb); sciences (read the introduction to Hurt); or humanities (read chapters 1 and 2 of Blazek and Aversa).

    a. Which chapter(s) covers your subject area?

    b. Under which heading(s) is your topic listed in the index?

    c. Is your specific topic covered or only the wider discipline within which it falls?

    d. Comment on the value of this source to your research.

3. *American Reference Books Annual* (latest edition and earlier editions if necessary): read the introduction.

    a. Which chapter covers your subject area?

    b. Under which heading(s) is your topic listed in the index?

    c. List any new titles on your topic that sound useful.

    d. Comment on the value of this source to your research.

SEARCH STRATEGY

For a hypothetical ten-page paper on a topic, students develop a search strategy and timeline (spanning one term).

Notes and Suggested Reading

1. "Serendipity," *Webster's New International Dictionary of the English Language*, 2nd ed. unabr. (Springfield, Mass.: Merriam, 1958).

2. Jean Ward and Kathleen A. Hansen, *Search Strategies in Mass Communication* (New York: Longman, 1987), p. 16.

3. A bibliographic essay on "Search Strategy Models" is included in Dorothy B. Lilley and Rose Marie Badough, *Library and Information Science: A Guide to Information Sources*, Books, Publishing, and Libraries Information Guide Series, Vol. 5 (Detroit, Mich.: Gale, 1982), pp. 17–22.

4. A similar strategy is described in Sarah Barbara Watstein and Stan Nash, "Researching 'Hot' Topics in the Social Sciences," *Research Strategies* 1:77–82 (Spring 1983).

5. Marcia J. Bates, "Information Search Tactics," *Journal of the American Society for Information Science* 30:205–214 (July 1979). In this article, Bates delineates twenty-nine tactics in four categories: monitoring, file structure, search formulation, and term tactics.

In a subsequent article, she offers seventeen "idea tactics" for solving research problems: think, brainstorm, meditate, consult, rescue, wander, catch, break, breach, reframe, notice, jolt, change, focus, dilate, skip, stop. Marcia J. Bates, "Idea Tactics," *Journal of the American Society for Information Science* 30:280–289 (Sept. 1979).

6. *Readers Advisory Service: Selected Topical Booklists* (New York: Science Associates, 1974–); *CPL Bibliography* (Chicago: Council of Planning Librarians, 1959–); *LC Science Tracer Bullets* (Washington, D.C.: Reference Section, Science and Technology Division, Library of Congress, 1972–); *Annual Review of Anthropology* (Palo Alto, Calif.: Annual Reviews, 1972–); *Communication Yearbook* (Newbury Park, Calif.: Sage, 1977–).

7. Jon Lindgren, "The Idea of Evidence in Bibliographic Inquiry," in *Theories of Bibliographic Education: Designs for Teaching*, eds. Cerise Oberman and Katina Strauch (New York: Bowker, 1982), pp. 27–46.

8. Peter Allison, "Stalking the Elusive Grey Literature," *College and Research Libraries News* 48:244–246 (May 1987). Allison uses the adjective "grey" as a synonym for "fugitive" and cautions against confusing those terms with "ephemera." *The ALA Glossary of Library and Information Science* (Chicago: American Library Assn., 1983) provides the following definitions:

> Fugitive: Material printed in limited quantities and usually of immediate interest at the time of, or in place of, publication, such as pamphlets, programs, and processed publications.
>
> Ephemera: 1. Materials of transitory interest and value, consisting generally of pamphlets or clippings which are usually kept for a limited time in vertical files. 2. Similar materials of the past which have acquired literary or historical significance.

9. Joel Rudd and Mary Jo Rudd, "Coping with Information Load: User Strategies and Implications for Librarians," *College and Research Libraries* 47:315–322 (July 1986).

10. Eugene P. Sheehy, ed., *Guide to Reference Books*, 10th ed. (Chicago: American Library Assn., 1986). Other guides include William H. Webb et al., *Sources of Information in the Social Sciences*, 3rd ed. (Chicago: American Library Assn., 1986); Charlie Deuel Hurt, *Information Sources in Science and Technology* (Englewood, Colo.: Libraries Unlimited, 1988); and Ron Blazek and Elizabeth Aversa, *The Humanities: A Selective Guide to Information Sources*, 3rd ed. (Englewood, Colo.: Libraries Unlimited, 1988).

11. Bohdan S. Wynar, *American Reference Books Annual* (Littleton, Colo.: Libraries Unlimited, 1970–   ).

Chapter *7*

Organizational Techniques

Library research is a detailed, complex, and time-consuming process. Students often fail to anticipate the amount of time and variety of skills that are necessary to conduct effective research. Techniques to organize the procedure, such as the search strategy and timeline discussed in chapter 6, as well as an outline and index cards, enhance the entire process.

Library research includes four stages: descriptive exploration, data collection, assimilation and application. A preliminary thesis and outline are results of the descriptive exploration. As the researcher's understanding of the topic deepens with the gathering of information, the thesis and outline are modified, refined, or perhaps significantly altered. The researcher develops a final thesis and outline while assimilating the information gathered. The thesis and outline, then, serve to guide and focus both the search for information and the application of that information in the written report.

A complete and careful record of the search for information is essential. Documentation provides a record of sources consulted (i.e., the bibliographic structure of the topic), and note taking provides a record of the data collected (i.e., the information structure of the topic).

Developing the Thesis and Outline

The thesis is the kernel of the written report or the whole point of the report in a nutshell. The outline is the thesis expanded into a listing of all the points which are outgrowths of the thesis.

As discussed in chapter 6, it is often useful to pose the preliminary thesis as a research question: the focus of the search for information.

A question, as opposed to a statement, promotes an open, questioning attitude and a willingness to look at all sides. It reinforces the process of research as discovering one's stance rather than corroborating one's preconceptions. The final thesis statement, however, should be phrased as a clear and thoughtful assertion. The substance of the preliminary thesis is also likely to change over the course of research as the student's understanding of and attitude towards the topic evolves.

Most students will need to do some background reading on a subject before developing a research question. Once an overview of the subject has been made and key concepts identified, the researcher can apply creative problem-solving techniques to formulate a research question. The student might list various features or aspects of the subject (such as time period, geographical location, events, issues, stances, implications, groups or individuals involved, and interested disciplines) and list alternatives under each category. Then the student can combine several of the options to create a research question. (This approach is illustrated in the recommended problem formulation activity at the end of this chapter.)

The final thesis is usually shaped when the researcher has finished collecting data and is assimilating the information. A clear perspective and central point are likely to emerge as the student reviews note cards and responds to the information gathered (see chapter 16, "The Assimilation and Application of Information"). As James Lester notes, the final thesis should fulfill several objectives:

1. It expresses your position in a full, declarative sentence, which is not a question, not a statement of purpose, and not merely a topic.
2. It limits the subject to a narrow focus that grows out of research.
3. It establishes an investigative, inventive edge to your research and thereby gives a reason for all your work.
4. It points forward to the conclusion.
5. It conforms to your note card evidence and your title.[1]

A preliminary outline lists aspects of the focused topic which will be researched. Like the thesis, the outline will be revised and refined as the search progresses: what is known about the topic at the outset of data collection naturally will be different from what is understood at the conclusion. The final outline will list the points that "prove" the thesis, and it should be a direct reflection of the thesis, i.e., a logical expansion of the concepts implicit in the thesis statement.

To develop a preliminary outline, students list all the thoughts they have about the topic so far. Ideas should be jotted down quickly in the order they occur. Clustering may be useful to stimulate free association (see chapter 5). Then the list or cluster is studied for patterns, natural groupings, and a logical organization. It may be easier to arrange and rearrange thoughts if they are written on separate pieces of paper.

Students group the ideas under general categories and then determine how to order the categories and the points within each category. Students will probably discover that some thoughts do not fit in and there are gaps in the coverage of the subject. Adjustments can be made to the preliminary outline at this point; the researcher will continue to modify and refine the outline as the search progresses.

When a preliminary or final outline is required with a research report, students should clarify the requirements for type and style of outline. The type of outline will be either topic or sentence, and it must be consistent throughout. Relationships between ideas are illustrated by the alphanumeric system and by indentation. Headings that are labelled with Roman numerals and capital letters and positioned closer to the left margin should be broader and more categorical than the more specific headings labelled with Arabic numerals and lower-case letters that are positioned further from the left margin.

While the preliminary outline is used to guide the data collection, the final outline is used to focus and organize the written report. A variety of organizational styles is possible, including chronological, cause and effect, or general to particular. The final outline is a result of revisions made to the preliminary outline during data collection and assimilation of the information gathered.

Computer software is available for generating ideas and developing outlines, as well as for formatting footnotes and bibliographies and creating note files. The campus computing center is likely to provide commercial or in-house software for such functions. A current source for identifying computer software is the quarterly *Consumer's Index to Product Evaluations and Information Sources*, which includes a section on computer hardware and software.

Keeping a Record of the Search

Careful documentation of a search fosters a systematic approach and can alleviate many of the frustrations of library research. There are as many approaches to documentation and note taking as there are research guides, and computer applications multiply the options. Library researchers must cite sources according to a style manual, keep a record of the search, and record information. In a technologically ideal situation, these functions, as well as access to information, would all be computerized. However, for the undergraduate researcher, manual methods of record keeping will be the norm for some time, and familiarity with manual documentation and note taking will aid the future researcher who computerizes these tasks.

The late-night kitchen table or bedroom floor sprawl consists of notes scribbled on notebook paper, scrap paper, and napkins, as well as books and photocopies themselves. Rather than these items, which must be searched repeatedly to develop each main point and then scrutinized to glean whatever information may be available for footnotes and a list of references, index cards are recommended because they are uniform and sturdy, and they can be easily arranged and rearranged. Figure 13 illustrates suggested formats for bibliography (bib) and content (note) cards using $3'' \times 5''$ and $4'' \times 6''$ index cards.

Citations on bib cards should be formatted according to the desired style manual at the time they are recorded. This approach necessitates keeping the style manual at hand and may seem to take more time when writing out the cards, but time is saved later during the final preparations, when every minute seems to count. Since the information must be copied onto the cards anyway, it is usually worth the time saved later to correctly format the citations at the outset, rather than rewriting them later.

In addition to a standard citation of the item and an annotation, the researcher may find it useful to record four additional elements of information: the source of the citation, location notes, whether the item includes a bibliography, and whether any information was taken from the source.

The source of the citation indicates where the researcher found the item listed; the source may be a catalog, bibliography, index, footnote, or, sometimes, an individual who recommended the item. The citing source can be abbreviated on the card; the subject heading and year searched under are worth noting as well. The source of the citation is an important record to have because no matter how careful and systematic a researcher is, some citations will likely be copied down incompletely or incorrectly. In that event, it is easy to verify the citation when the source is known. Some interlibrary loan request forms also ask for this information. The source of citation also may be useful should the researcher need to fill in gaps. If one item on an incomplete aspect of the topic has already been identified, the researcher may be able to go back to the source of that citation to identify additional items.

Bibliography (Bib) Card

	+	Indication of usefulness.
1	Roth, Audrey J. The Research Paper : Process, Form and Content. 6th ed. Belmont, Calif. : Wadsworth, 1989.	1. Example for citing a book. 2. Where did you find this item? 3. Call number, location, date of search, recall etc.
2	source of citation :	4. Does the item list additional sources?
3	location notes :	
4	bibliography included :	
5	note cards made :	5. Did you take notes or photocopy sections?

Brief annotation (descriptive or evaluative comments) on back. The comment should enable you to remember this item when looking at the bib card in the future.

Content (Note) Card

heading	Subtopic corresponding to topic.
A note may be a summary (concise abstract in your own words), paraphrase (the original passage translated into your own words), direct quote (copied exactly), personal comment (your own thought), or combination (note the source and distinguish between your own thought and an author's).	Abbreviated citation should include page number; refer to corresponding bib card for complete citation.
Roth, Resrch Paper...., pp. 122 - 129	

Only one item of information per card. Cards can then be arranged by headings to follow outline.

Figure 13. Bibliography and note cards

The location notes provide a record of the search for the item. If the citation is found in a library's catalog or serials list, the location and call number are entered. If the item is located on the shelf, a check is added. If the item is not located, "not on shelf" or "N.O.S." and the date are noted. If the item is recalled or traced, that should be noted along with the date, or if the item is requested through interlibrary loan. This kind of information is especially important in long-term research, for students may wonder after some period of time why they have not yet seen a potentially useful source. One glance at the bib card will reveal what steps have been taken and how long ago; the researcher can then determine how best to follow up.

Another useful bit of information to add to the bib card is whether the item includes a bibliography. The value of bibliographies and footnotes as a research tactic was noted in chapter 6. Bibliographies are also useful for filling in gaps. If a source that covers an incomplete area and that includes a bibliography has already been identified, the researcher may be able to quickly identify additional sources. On the bib card, it is important to note not only that the item includes a bibliography, but also whether additional bib cards have been made from that bibliography, i.e., whether the bibliography has already been researched.

Finally, students may wish to note what they have done with the content of the item—whether note cards were made or the item was photocopied. When writing a citation on a bibliography card, the researcher can easily and quickly format the card to add these four additional elements of information. They might be abbreviated as "src:," "loc:," "bib:," and "note:."

Annotating is a highly useful research and critical thinking skill. An annotation is added to the bib card so that the researcher can recall the item and identify specific sources that offered some particular contribution to the topic. When annotations are thoughtfully developed, the researcher both distills the essence of the item and formulates a personal response to it.

Annotations should characterize and assess. The researcher states the central idea or purpose of the work, comments on the overall quality of the item, and notes its usefulness for the topic. The researcher will also do well to describe the author's frame of reference.[2] Although annotations are typically only a couple of sentences or sentence fragments, they usually require a surprising degree of thought and consideration. Longer annotations are more accurately termed abstracts.

The bib cards can first be arranged for systematic searching of the library's holdings in card or online catalogs and serials list. Next they can be ordered by location or call number for item retrieval, and then sorted by items found and those not available. Cards for the items found can be divided into piles of useful and useless materials, and perhaps marked as such, using a symbol or color mark or notch. In long-term research, no bib cards should be discarded, as the researcher may encounter additional references to the same item, and it is easier to check one's cards than to duplicate a search out of uncertainty. Ultimately, the cards will be arranged alphabetically by author (or title, where there is no author) for the final list of references.

In a similar manner, the note cards will be progressively arranged. At the outset of research, the student is likely to take notes with only a vague sense of how, where, or whether they will actually be incorporated into the final report. That is why it is important to write only one point, fact, or thought onto each card—so that the information can be easily manipulated.

Note cards should include the researcher's own thoughts, reactions, and points as well as information copied and summarized from other sources. Once enough information has been gathered to develop a working outline, headings from the outline can be added to the note cards. The end goal is to arrange the note cards in the order of the outline and write the paper by working through the stack of cards.

It is critical to include the source on every note card, even when the information is summarized, and to be sure that summaries are not mere paraphrasings. Undergraduates are rarely "experts" in an area they may research. Especially when working from a limited knowledge base, scrupulous documentation is preferable to unintentional plagiarism.

Some students may enter citations and notes into a computer file for sorting, generating lists, and other manipulation. A variety of database management programs is available, or word-processing programs can be adapted to this function by creating and duplicating a format or template. Learning manual note taking will enhance the students' transition to computerized applications, and, until lap-top computers are common, researchers will remain dependent on manual techniques when they work away from the computer.

A search strategy and timeline are used to structure the research process; the 'organizational techniques of outlining and record keeping, whether manual or computerized, focus the search and capture the results.

Sample Learning Objectives

Concepts to understand:

Functions of the preliminary and final thesis statements and outlines—how they differ and why.

The value of index cards for recording sources and information.
The nature of annotations.
Formatting bibliography cards.
Organizing note cards.

Skills to apply:

Developing a research question.
Developing a preliminary outline.
Using a style manual to format a citation.
Using different notetaking styles.

Sample Class Discussion Questions

1. Recount how you organized your last research project. What difficulties did you encounter at the outset, in the middle, at the end?
2. In retrospect, how would you organize that project differently?
3. What notetaking methods have you used in research?
4. How have you used those notes to write a research paper?
5. What are the conventions of outlining?
6. Why is an outline likely to change as the research progresses?
7. What is a research question and how does it differ from a thesis?
8. What are the objectives of a thesis?
9. What is an annotation? An abstract?
10. Why should you annotate your bibliography cards?
11. How can you verify an incomplete or incorrect citation?
12. When should you footnote?
13. What is plagiarism?

Recommended Problem Formulation Activity

The way a problem is stated or conceptualized may exert some influence on the solution and on the pertinent information which is gathered.[3]

A problem is half solved if it is properly stated.[4]

The mere formulation of a problem is far more often more essential than its solution, which may be merely a matter of mathematical or experimental skill. To raise new questions, new possibilities, to regard old problems from a new angle requires creative imagination and marks real advances in science.[5]

These three quotations underline the significance of problem formulation in research. The way a problem or topic is articulated determines the research strategy and influences the results of the search. As central as it is to the research process, problem formulation is typically a problem in itself for undergraduate researchers. They often come to the library before focusing their purpose or translating an instructor's requirements into a workable approach. The following activity provides an excellent structure for students to formulate a research question as a preliminary thesis.[6]

The format of this activity is a "learning cycle" or "three-step process which presents subject content in a structure explicitly designed to promote the use of self-regulation." In the exploration stage, students learn a new concept by applying previous experience to discover new patterns and relationships. In the second stage, clarification of the new concept is provided and students apply a new skill through invention. Finally, students use an application to their own topics to reinforce the new concepts.

The learning cycle for problem formulation is done in small groups. Each group receives a packet of the same cards. The activity requires forty-five to seventy-five minutes for completion. The third application stage can be assigned as a follow-up take-home assignment.

LEARNING CYCLE

Questions (appearing on individual cards):

The current gas shortage has been caused by America's overconsumption. Do you agree or disagree?

How much rainfall did Charleston receive in May 1976?

Define a "Hippogriff."

Recently, the U.S. Congress passed a law which put aside thousands of acres of land in Alaska as wilderness areas. How much land is involved and who was responsible for introducing this legislation?

In what state is the Hudson River located?

Compare the number of deaths in the United States attributed to homicide, automobile accidents, and heart attacks.

Is there a relationship between unemployment and recession?

The concept of "Manifest Destiny" was often cited as an excuse for the destruction and removal of the Indian nations during the period of this country's western expansion. Explore the issue.

How many nuclear power plants are in the United States?

Exploration. Each card in your packet has a research problem written on it. Sort the cards into two piles (sets) according to the *type of answer* you would need to satisfy the question.

State how the cards in each pile resemble each other and how they are different.

Pile 1:

Pile 2:

Invention. You have identified two distinct types of questions using the process of *question analysis*. The two types of questions you have identified are factual and conceptual. These terms are most often applied to sentence structure, but in question analysis they take on slightly different meaning.

The factual question asks only for facts and therefore requires the use of fact tools, e.g., statistical sources, directories, etc.

The conceptual question asks for both facts and concepts; facts alone will not satisfy the question. Intermediary tools must be used to locate information, e.g., the card [or online] catalog will locate books, periodical indexes will locate periodical literature.

1. Before beginning research on a conceptual question you must be aware of the various components that can help you focus your research problem. Although you can now recognize the types of questions that demand research, it is to your advantage to be able to focus your search. The chart below lists four broad areas that can assist you in focusing your problem.

2. Select one conceptual problem from your packet of cards. Using the chart below, list all the possible variables from which you can choose to narrow your topic.

Geography	Interest Groups	Time Period	Implications

3. What broad subject areas or fields of study might this question involve?
4. By selecting one component from each list, rephrase the question into a focused research problem.

Application. You have just completed question reformulation. By identifying all the possible variables you have eliminated many areas of research by focusing on a specific area.

A typical chart, although it will vary from question to question, would be:

Geography	Time Span	Interest Groups	Implications	Disciplines
national	historical	women	health	sociology
international	current year	labor	economic	psychology
regional	specific event	adolescents	political	environmental studies
local	etc.	teachers	etc.	American history
specific place	---	politicians	---	Literature
etc.	---	a particular group	---	etc.
---	---	etc.	---	---

1. Using the research topic for this course analyze your question by charting all the possibilities which apply to your topic. Be specific (e.g., specify U.S. instead of national).
2. Reformulate your research problem into a concise question.

Sample In-Class Activities

1. As a class or in small groups, students cluster on a topic and use the results to develop a research question and preliminary outline.
2. Distribute copies of card or online catalog records for books. Students, individually or in small groups, cite the items according to a designated style manual. They compare those records and subsequent citations to the actual books.
3. Distribute photocopies of a passage from a text. Individually, students write three different note cards: summarizing, paraphrasing, and responding to quotations taken from the passage. As a class or in small groups, students compare the results.

Sample Take-Home Exercise

For a given or selected topic, students take notes on an encyclopedia article, cite the article on a bib card, and develop a preliminary outline.

Notes and Suggested Reading

1. James D. Lester, *Writing Research Papers: A Complete Guide*, 5th ed. (Glenview, Ill.: Scott, Foresman, 1987), p. 83. See also Audrey J. Roth, *The Research Paper: Process, Form, and Content*, 6th ed. (Belmont, Calif.: Wadsworth, 1989), pp. 136–141.

2. Roth, *The Research Paper*, p. 258.

3. Charles K. West, *The Social and Psychological Distortion of Information* (Chicago: Nelson-Hall, 1981), p. 78.

4. John Dewey, quoted in Sidney J. Parnes, *Creative Behavior Guidebook* (New York: Scribner, 1967), p. 124.

5. Albert Einstein, quoted in Parnes, *Creative Behavior Guidebook*, p. 129.

6. Reprinted with permission from Cerise Oberman, "Question Analysis and the Learning Cycle," *Research Strategies* 1:22–30 (Winter 1983). Updated or more local issues can be substituted.

Chapter *8*

Vocabulary Control

At the very core of the research process are words. Researchers look for information with words, but few undergraduates pause to consider the meaning of this truism as they initiate a search for information, and rarely will they deliberately determine the best terms and combinations of terms for their topic. Libraries are systems that encode information, using subject headings and classification. The researcher must decode the system by identifying relevant headings and call numbers.

Researchers establish vocabulary control by identifying words, phrases, and subject headings to describe their topic and look for information on the subject. An initial step in the research process is to list the words that denote the topic, including synonymous, broader, narrower, and related terms. Brainstorming, encyclopedias, and word books are useful for this task. Vocabulary control is an ongoing process of articulation and translation; index cards are useful for keeping a record of which terms were tried and which were successful in each tool.

Researchers can also consult controlled vocabularies as well as catalogs and indexes to determine actual subject headings or descriptors. A controlled vocabulary is a collection of terms designated for use by a particular access source. Such thesauri may implicitly project a biased world view and influence the researcher's perception of a subject. Critical evaluation is useful for assessing the connotations inherent in indexing vocabularies and compensating for their deficiencies.

Articulation

Vocabulary control should be initiated early in the research process. As soon as a subject is selected, the student would do well to brainstorm or cluster on the concept to identify premises and stimulate speculation as well as to generate various ways of articulating or expressing the topic. From the start, the student should attempt to evoke synonymous, related, broader, and narrower terms. The very process of writing words down will usually elicit more terms.

The concept of vocabulary control is graphically reinforced when strategies are developed for online catalog and computer database searching. The format of the typical database searching worksheet (see also the "Search Strategy Worksheet" presented in chapter 6) and the relationships established with logical connectors, as well as electronic responses when the search is actually conducted, require students to focus vocabulary.

Applying the worksheet model, the student first analyzes the research question to identify concepts. Two to four concepts are optimum: a single concept indicates the topic is too general, and more than three or four concepts are usually unwieldy. Students should avoid designating as concepts terms that describe relationships between concepts, such as: "the result of," "the effects of," "the relationship between," "the development of," and "the analysis of." Such terms do not translate well into indexing language. Students often find it difficult though enlightening to approach their topic from the perspectives of indexing vocabularies as well as subject conceptualization.

Next, a list of terms is generated for each concept. Relevant words include synonyms as well as terms closely related to the concept. Each list should include a variety of broader and narrower terms as well, so that the researcher can select from an array of terms depending on the access source and its subject specificity. For example, in an index covering all the sciences or social sciences, the researcher will usually need to search under a more general term than may be necessary in an index covering a single or fewer disciplines.

Depending on their familiarity with the subject, students may be ready to develop a vocabulary control list before or after reading for background. Encyclopedia indexes and articles will probably suggest additional headings. General language dictionaries, thesauri, and subject dictionaries should also be consulted to develop a full list.

No matter how thoughtfully and carefully students establish vocabulary control at the outset, most will discover additional terms as the search progresses; these should be added to the list. Because headings may vary not only from source to source, but also from year to year within a particular source, the researcher is also well advised to create a separate vocabulary control list for each access source (and perhaps each year) consulted, listing all the terms tried, and marking the successful terms. Index cards serve this purpose, as do some computer programs. In long-term research especially, a researcher may forget whether or where a particular term was searched early on.

Translation: Controlled Vocabularies

Once the student has articulated concepts and terms to describe an information need, the research question must be translated into the indexing languages of access sources. This translation is accomplished by consulting controlled vocabularies. Controlled vocabulary "refers to index terms or classification codes that have been created to provide consistent and orderly description of the contents of documents or records."[1] Controlled vocabularies regulate selection from equivalent terms, the form of individual words, and the composition of phrases.

Most controlled vocabularies are published as a standardized list, often called a thesaurus. The conventional thesaurus is a listing of synonyms arranged alphabetically or according to a classification scheme, such as the well-known *Roget's Thesaurus*. There are also thesauri for subject areas.[2] A controlled vocabulary thesaurus is a list of subject headings or descriptors that may be assigned to items in a particular access source; it usually includes a cross-reference system. The *Library of Congress Subject Headings* is a controlled vocabulary for card and online catalogs. Some print indexes, such as the ERIC indexes for education and *Psychological Abstracts*, include thesauri. Many online index producers also publish their vocabularies (including ERIC, *Psych Info*, *Medline*, and *Chemical Abstracts*), and in most databases the vocabulary is searchable online.[3]

Bates identifies six different types of controlled vocabularies.[4] Such distinctions will be irrelevant for most undergraduate researchers, but the difference between subject headings and descriptors may be of some interest. The Library of Congress and most print indexes employ subject headings that describe an entire publication and may be subdivided. Descriptors are used in most online and CD-ROM indexes; they generally describe discrete concepts within a publication.[5] Typically, only a few subject headings, known as precoordinate indexing, are assigned to an item, while a larger number of descriptors are usually used. Descriptors are postcoordinate because they are combined by the searcher using logical connectors (such as Boolean logic).

The formats of most controlled vocabulary lists are similar, and they include broader, narrower, and related terms, as well as indications of headings not used. The abbreviations used to designate each of these types of terms vary from thesaurus to thesaurus. Many thesauri include scope notes, which define terms as they are used in the vocabulary. Some sources will include additional lists of terms, such as the hierarchical tree structures in MeSH, and the ERIC rotated descriptor display, which provides a permuted alphabetical index of all words that form ERIC headings.

Controlled vocabularies are useful not only to determine the particular and precise terms to use when searching for information about a given topic, but also to identify the terminology of a subject area. The researcher can use a thesaurus to suggest a variety of terms for a topic and to discover aspects of a subject for focusing. Thesauri can be used to overview hierarchies and relationships among terms and concepts.

Several cross-reference listings analyze the relationships between multiple controlled vocabularies and between classification systems and subject headings. *Subject Authorities: A Guide to Subject Cataloging* (New York: Bowker, 1981) provides, in three volumes, a Subject Heading Index listing the Dewey Decimal and Library of Congress classification numbers for each LC heading; a Dewey Decimal Classification Index listing the LC heading and classification number for each DD number; and a Library of Congress Classification Index listing the LC heading and DD number for each LC number.

The *Subject Cross Reference Guide* (Princeton, N.J.: National Library Service, 1976) is an alphabetical listing, with variants and related subjects, of the most universally used subject headings from the *Readers' Guide to Periodical Literature*. The *Cross-Reference Index: A Subject Heading Guide* (New York: Bowker, 1974) lists subject headings from LCSH, Sears, *Readers' Guide*, the *New York Times Index*, the *Public Affairs Information Service*, and the *Business Periodicals Index*.

Other Approaches to Indexing

Natural language is used for subject access in some indexes. In most online databases it is possible to search free text—the researcher types in any terms to describe a topic and instructs the system to search in a variety of fields, including title, abstract, descriptor, and sometimes a free term field, which includes nonstandard indexing terms assigned by the indexer. In some cases, the full text of a document may be searched. Many online catalogs also allow searching by any words, in any order, in title, subject heading, or other fields.

A similar approach in some print indexes, such as *Biological Abstracts* and the ISI citation indexes, is keyword indexing. In this format, the researcher looks for words that are likely to have been used by authors in article titles on a topic. These are sometimes called KWIC (for keyword in context) indexes because they provide other words in the title as context for the searched term.

There are disadvantages and advantages to the natural language approach. In order to conduct a comprehensive search, the researcher must look under every term authors might use in titles on a topic. Titles that are not particularly descriptive, especially the allusive or metaphoric titles common in the humanities, will be missed. However, controlled vocabularies are rulebound, they tend to be conservative and static, and they often fail to accommodate emerging areas and newly coined terms. Natural language offers access with the terms most commonly and currently in use. It also allows the researcher to focus on identifying terms without worrying about the order or format of words in a term.

The Access Source as Thesaurus

Catalogs and indexes themselves can be consulted to penetrate the controlled vocabularies upon which they are based. The researcher can look for cross-references, check synonyms, and observe changes in the vocabulary over time.[6] In a card catalog, the subject tracings at the bottom of the cards can be used as references to additional headings. Online catalog records typically include tracings, and some online catalogs will display their authority control as well. Most print indexes include *see* references. Computer databases generally provide online access to their controlled vocabulary. The records in most online indexes include a descriptor field, equivalent to subject tracings. These approaches may be critical when no separately published thesaurus is available, but they are also useful to support and double-check the results of using a print thesaurus. Even practiced researchers are likely to discover headings in the access sources that eluded them in the thesauri.

The Politics of Language and Controlled Vocabularies

Depending on the topic, subject headings and descriptors may ease or hinder the researcher's access to information. Index terms may provide direct and comprehensive access to a topic, or they may be inconsistent, imprecise, and value-laden, scattering information and overlaying connotations. Index terms may be precisely descriptive, with most relevant materials listed under a limited number of headings, or they may be too general or peripheral, necessitating the use of a large number of headings that call up a burdensome amount of irrelevant items.

As noted in chapter 10, words are not value-free. In this era of sustained insistence upon human rights, many individuals are highly sensitive to words that reinforce the denial of equity and suppression of diversity. When particular words or phrasings are selected over others, individuals who impute negative connotations to the selected terms may be offended. Taken as a whole, a controlled vocabulary may reflect a particular bias or world view.

The *Library of Congress Subject Headings* is a case in point. An argument can be made that this controlled vocabulary maintains a white, Western, Christian, male perspective. For example, although WASPs (Persons) is listed as a subject heading, it is associated with only five broader terms (including European Americans and Protestants—United States) and no subdivisions. In contrast, Afro-Americans, Asian Americans, Hispanic Americans, and Indians of North America are each associated with a large number and variety of subdivisions and included in an extensive selection of phrases, such as:

AFRO-AMERICANS—DANCING
AFRO-AMERICANS IN THE PROFESSIONS
ASIAN AMERICAN FAMILIES
ASIAN AMERICANS IN BUSINESS
HISPANIC AMERICANS—FOOD
HISPANIC AMERICAN YOUTH
INDIANS OF NORTH AMERICA—ALCOHOL USE
INDIANS OF NORTH AMERICA AS SOLDIERS

The implication seems to be that such designations are not required for the white population because WASPs are the norm, and that headings for dancing, professions, family, and so on refer exclusively to the white population unless otherwise indicated. The same pattern can be observed for other ethnic groups, religions other than Christian, and women. Also, generic male designations are still used in *LCSH*, such as Man for the anthropological human and for the theological humankind.

LCSH is a source that librarians love to hate: it includes numerous examples of offensive, bizarre, and archaic headings. Literary warrant is often claimed as justification: headings only reflect the literature they index. The difficulty with this justification is that literatures are developmental, changing with the conditions that produce them, while indexing languages are slow to reflect changes. As a tool, *LCSH* may be merely less than helpful and rather annoying, or it can be viewed as inappropriate and misleading. As the most widely used controlled vocabulary in U.S. academic libraries, it affects the research of many library users.

Researchers must apply creative problem solving and critical thinking to compensate for controlled vocabulary deficiencies. They should brainstorm to generate additional terms every time they encounter a dead end or an unsatisfactory yield. They should identify their own and social biases and attempt to conceptualize the topic from alternative perspectives. A variety of controlled vocabulary and subject thesauri should be studied whenever possible, as well as the access sources. The literature itself should be read with an eye to terminology. Researchers should not assume that the obvious and readily identified terms are the only ones available or possible, or that the indexing vocabulary is value-free or unbiased.[7]

The nature and quality of subject access will determine to a significant degree the course and effectiveness of a search for information. Subject headings and descriptors determine the accessibility of information, the researcher's perception of what is available, and, perhaps, the researcher's understanding of and attitude towards the subject. Researchers must practice critical awareness to assess and compensate for the deficiencies of subject access.

Sample Learning Objectives

Concepts to understand:

> The articulation of research topics as searchable concepts and terms.
> The translation of research topics into indexing languages.
> The structure of controlled vocabularies.
> The use of natural language or subject access in keyword indexes and most online databases.
> The use of access sources themselves as thesauri.
> The political nature of language and the projection of bias in controlled vocabularies.

Skills to apply:

> Using brainstorming to generate terms for a concept.
> Keeping a vocabulary control list or cards during a search for information.
> Using controlled vocabularies to expand vocabulary control.
> Using natural language to search by keyword or free text.
> Using access sources to expand vocabulary control.
> Identifying a variety of perspectives on a topic to become aware of the potential for bias.

Sample Class Discussion Questions

1. What is vocabulary control? Why is it important in research?
2. What is a concept?
3. What are synonyms?
4. Why will you need both broader and narrower terms when looking for information?
5. What are some reference sources that may be useful for developing vocabulary control?
6. Why should you keep an ongoing record of your vocabulary control?
7. What does a thesaurus do?
8. What is the difference between a subject heading and a descriptor?
9. What is free-text searching?
10. What is a KWIC index?
11. How do access sources help you with vocabulary control?
12. What are some value-laden terms?
13. What are some words with negative connotations?
14. How could a controlled vocabulary project a world view?
15. Why does *LCSH* include offensive, bizarre, and outdated terms?
16. How can you compensate for the deficiencies of controlled vocabularies?

Sample In-Class Activities

1. Suggest a cross-disciplinary subject (such as suicide or alcoholism) to the class. As a class, develop a research question about

the subject, separate the question into concepts, and brainstorm a list of terms for each concept. Divide the class into small groups, and assign each group a controlled vocabulary (including *LCSH*, *Thesaurus of Psychological Index Terms*, *Thesaurus of Sociological Indexing Terms*, and *Thesaurus of ERIC Descriptors*). The small groups continue to develop vocabulary control for the topic using the assigned thesaurus, and then each group reports back to the class at large to compile a master list. As a class, note and discuss variations in terminology and focus among the disciplines represented.

2. Working individually or in small groups, students receive a page photocopied from *LCSH* (or another controlled vocabulary) and a set of questions to answer about the entries. For example, the following questions are based on page 1308 (Family) of the eleventh edition of *LCSH*:

> What is the official heading for Family and television?
> What is the heading for Family folklore?
> What is the heading for Family recreation?
> What are some headings for racial or ethnic families in the United States?
> What is the heading for White families?
> What term is not used for Family corporations?
> What is a broader term for Family day care?
> What is a related term for Family allowances?
> What is a narrower term for Family—Research?
> What term is used for Family counseling?
> Under what types of headings may Family be used as a subdivision?

3. In small groups, students look in *LCSH* and other controlled vocabularies for headings concerning racial or ethnic groups, women, homosexuals, or controversial subjects. Students report back to the class on the nature of the access and perceived biases.

Sample Take-Home Exercises

1. Students create a thesaurus entry for a subject by listing terms in each of the following categories:

Synonymous
Related
Broader
Narrower

2. Students create a vocabulary control worksheet for a topic, using the search term format in figure 12 (p. 78). For each term, students indicate whether it was derived from brainstorming, a controlled vocabulary, or an access source. They list the thesauri and indexes consulted.
3. Students use *LCSH* (or another controlled vocabulary) to develop a list of indexing terms for a topic.

SAMPLE DIRECTIONS FOR *LCSH*

Look for your subject in the *Library of Congress Subject Headings* (*LCSH*). Begin with the most specific expression of your topic, then broaden, narrow, and pursue synonyms as appropriate. Remember that only a few proper nouns are included as examples. Make a list of established headings and look up in *LCSH* the relevant broader, related, and narrower terms listed. Compile a list of headings in priority order for looking them up in the catalogs. Your list should consist of one heading followed by another, with no symbols, abbreviations, or indentations. If you include subdivisions, list the complete heading: heading, dash, subdivision.

For example, if your topic was the use of mass communication by religious groups, you might begin by looking under MASS COMMUNICATION. You would discover that this term is not an established heading, but MASS MEDIA is. Looking at the subdivisions under MASS MEDIA you should note the subdivision—RELIGIOUS ASPECTS, as well as the narrower term MASS MEDIA IN RELIGION. Perusing the narrower terms, you might note LOCAL MASS MEDIA. Browsing through the MASS MEDIA phrase headings, you would discover MASS MEDIA IN RELIGION again, this time with accompanying references. Everything included in that entry would be worth looking up for additional headings.

Note UF (used for) terms and any additional terms that occur to you as you work on this assignment. Although they are not "official" subject headings, you may wish to search for them as words in titles.

Do not use capitals, punctuation, prepositions or conjunctions when you enter words in the online catalog; you may enter words in any order.

Your list to submit should look like this:

Subject: The use of mass communication by religious groups

Official LCSH

> MASS MEDIA IN RELIGION
> RELIGIOUS BROADCASTING
> RELIGIOUS NEWSPAPERS AND PERIODICALS
> JOURNALISM, RELIGIOUS
> MOVING-PICTURES IN CHURCH WORK
> MASS MEDIA—RELIGIOUS ASPECTS
> COMMUNICATION—RELIGIOUS ASPECTS
> ADVERTISING—CHURCHES
> LOCAL MASS MEDIA

Other Possibilities

> RELIGIOUS COMMUNICATION
> CHRISTIAN COMMUNICATION
> RELIGION AND MASS COMMUNICATION
> FILM IN RELIGION
> TELEVISION IN RELIGION
> RADIO IN RELIGION

Notes and Suggested Reading

1. Marcia J. Bates, "How to Use Controlled Vocabularies More Effectively in Online Searching," *Online* 12:46 (Nov. 1988).

2. Two recent examples of thesauri are Samuel R. Brown, comp., *Finding the Source in Sociology and Anthropology: A Thesaurus-Index to the Reference Collection*, Finding the Source, no. 1 (New York: Greenwood, 1987) and Mary Ellen S. Capek, ed., *A Women's Thesaurus: An Index of Language Used to Describe and Locate Information by and about Women* (New York: Harper, 1987).

3. For an extensive listing of database thesauri, see Lois Mai Chan and Richard Pollard, *Thesauri Used in Online Databases: An Analytical Guide* (New York: Greenwood, 1988).

4. Bates, "How to Use Controlled Vocabularies More Effectively in Online Searching."

5. For a discussion of the failure of the eleventh edition of *LCSH* to recognize this distinction, see Mary Dykstra, "LC Subject Headings Disguised as a Thesaurus," *Library*

Journal 113:42–46 (1 Mar. 1988), and Mary Dykstra, "Can Subject Headings Be Saved?" *Library Journal* 113:55–58 (15 Sept. 1988).

6. James Benson and Ruth Kay Maloney, "Principles of Searching," *RQ* 14:319 (Summer 1975).

7. For a case study of one student's experience when seeking information out of the mainstream (i.e., inventions of blacks), see Mary M. Huston in collaboration with Joe L. Williams, "Researcher Response to the Politics of Information," *Research Strategies* 5:90–93 (Spring 1987).

Chapter 9

Identifying, Locating, and Evaluating Books

Books are the archetypal information format; in fact, the library means books to most students. Undergraduates typically initiate library research by looking for books, the most obvious and familiar of sources, as there is something comforting about being able to take home such a weighty publication on a subject. However, researchers should consider the nature and value of books in order to incorporate them appropriately in research.

Books on a research topic can be identified by consulting card and online catalogs as well as bibliographies. Bibliographies are important for identifying what has been published on a topic other than what may be available in a particular library. The card catalog has long been the mainstay of research and bibliographic instruction, but in this decade it has been replaced in most academic libraries by computerized access. In many libraries the transition from manual to automated access is incomplete, and, to a greater or lesser extent, researchers will need to use both modes.

In the classroom, the ratio of card to online coverage and the order in which the two modes are introduced will depend on the extent of the transition to computerization in the particular library. Introducing students first to the basic principles underlying the card catalog is useful to prepare them both to use that approach and to better understand the advantages and disadvantages of the online method. However, where the online catalog has become the principal mode of access, it should probably be introduced first because students are likely to find the computerized version of far greater interest and research value.

Identifying Books

Chapter 6 defines a research strategy as "an overall plan of action," while search tactics are "discrete operations to further the search at specific points within it." Strategies are also useful for approaching different types of sources; the researcher might develop strategies for locating background information, books, newspapers, periodical articles, government publications, and so on. Each strategy would include specific tactics to overcome difficulties. To develop a strategy for identifying and locating books, the researcher must determine the coverage of the access tool in the particular library, potential search terms, and the adequacy of the library collection for the research topic.

Increasing numbers of libraries are automating their catalogs. When both manual and computerized catalogs are available, researchers need to know what is included and excluded in each, both in terms of time periods and types of material. While card catalogs have consistently provided access by author, title, and subject, online catalogs vary in the types of access available as well as in the procedures for using the available search modes. Before approaching a catalog to identify books, the researcher should develop a vocabulary control list by consulting the *Library of Congress Subject Headings*. Since most online systems also offer free text searching (by words in titles and other fields), the researcher will also want to brainstorm and perhaps consult thesauri to generate a list of keywords for searching.

The researcher may need to develop tactics if the search results are not satisfactory. If too many cards or records are encountered, narrower headings or terms can be tried. Conversely, when too few cards or records result, broader headings or terms may be needed. The first attempt may indicate that the subject will require focus or suggest possibilities for narrowing. The researcher may discover that a particular topic must be approached less directly than expected. For example, one student looking for books on the sixteenth-century English navy found that the correct heading was GREAT BRITAIN—HISTORY, NAVAL—TUDORS, 1485–1603.

An initial catalog search may reveal the extent of the library's collection in the subject area. If the coverage appears inadequate for the researcher's purpose, the student can decide whether to change topics, to seek other types of materials, or to expand the strategy to include identifying books through bibliographies and catalogs of special collections in order to request items through interlibrary loan.

THE CARD CATALOG

In libraries that are not automated, the card catalog serves as the index to a library's book collection. It can be said that a card catalog lists the books, the whole books, and nothing but the books, for card catalogs do not typically analyze the contents of books, nor do they include materials such as periodicals, newspapers, government publications, audiovisual materials, manuscript collections, or maps. Card catalogs may be "divided," usually into two alphabetical sections for author-title and subject, or "dictionary," with all cards interfiled into one alphabetical arrangement. No matter the arrangement, there are three basic approaches to finding materials: author, title, and subject.

Students generally think of an author in the narrow sense of the person who wrote a book. In terms of cataloging, the author is whoever is responsible for the intellectual content of a book. The author may be a group or corporate body, such as a government, society, or institution. Corporate authors include committees, departments, bureaus, or other subdivisions of an organization. Corporate names take many forms and may be filed under a geographic or political unit.

The card for the author is generally designated as the main entry. The majority of main entries are under the personal author, but they are sometimes under corporate author, editor, or title. The main entry card may be the only card for a given book that lists all editions of the work or includes all location notes. All cards other than the main entry are called added entries and may include headings for editor, compiler, translator, added authors, title, series, and various subjects.

The title approach is useful when the researcher does not know the author's name or its spelling. The title approach may also be used to find books that do not have an individual author, such as anthologies, the Bible, or the *World Almanac*. The subject approach is used to find books about a particular topic.

Subject access to the card catalog is controlled by the *Library of Congress Subject Headings*, discussed in chapter 8, "Vocabulary Control." Because many researchers find the LC list is inconsistent and illogical and favors a white, Western, male perspective, students must be urged to use it carefully and alerted to the potential difficulties in seeking sources on subjects that do not fit neatly into the designated headings.

Authority control in general is a tricky business for catalogers. For example, it is sometimes difficult to determine the correct form of an author's name, especially when a writer has used one or more pseudonyms. *See* references could be used to alleviate such problems, but they are costly to establish and maintain. Cataloging rules and subject headings are slow to change, and confusion is often compounded when old and new forms exist simultaneously in a catalog. The result is a complex tool that requires training and practice to exploit fully.

Because most catalog records are generated by the Library of Congress, researchers can expect some degree of consistency from library to library. The bibliographic elements of a catalog card should already be familiar to most undergraduates, but many may not recognize the technical description, notes, or tracings. The latter is particularly useful for expanding vocabulary control.

Researchers can often discover new terms to look under by checking subject tracings. The author or title card for a particular book that is useful for a topic can be looked up to determine its tracings. Researchers can also check the tracings on the subject cards to discover even more related headings.

The arrangement of cards in the catalog is complex and governed by detailed filing rules. Most catalogs are arranged word by word rather than letter by letter. The distinction is important because it applies to any alphabetically arranged work, including indexes, encyclopedias, and phone books.

Word by word means that the arrangement is alphabetical by words, and the spaces between words are taken into consideration. For example, "land grant" would precede "landfall." Word by word filing proceeds letter by letter to the end of each word, at which point the blank space is counted. In this arrangement, it is as if the alphabet had twenty-seven elements, the first of which is a blank space: blank space, A, B, C, D, and so on. The blank space in "New York" means it is filed before "Newark."

Letter by letter means that the spaces between the words are ignored. In this arrangement, "landfall" would precede "land grant." Letter by letter alphabetization proceeds letter by letter with no regard for the ends of words and the blanks between—as if everything ran together. Under letter by letter, "New York" is filed after "Newark."

Following is an example of how terms are alphabetized under the two arrangements:

Word by Word	*Letter by Letter*
New Amsterdam	New Amsterdam
New Mexico	Newark
New York	New Mexico
Newark	Newton, Isaac
Newton, Isaac	New York

Because alphabetization is not as easy as "A, B, C," a few other filing rules are worth noting. A word with multiple applications is filed in the order of first person, then place, and finally thing. For example:

Glasgow, Ellen	(Person)
Glasgow, Scotland	(Place)
Glasgow. [title]	(Thing: a title is considered to be a thing.)

While punctuation and articles at the beginning of titles are usually ignored, abbreviations and numerals in titles may be spelled out. Initialisms (such as C.I.A. and U.S.A., which are sounded as letters) typically appear before words beginning with the same letter, but acronyms (such as UNESCO and NASA, which are sounded as words) are often interfiled as words. Names beginning with *M'*, *Mc*, or *Mac* may be arranged as if spelled *Mac* and then interfiled with words that begin with the letters *mac*, such as machine.

Subject headings can be subdivided by form, topic, geographical entity, or time period. Form subdivisions describe the intellectual form of the material (BIBLIOGRAPHIES, DICTIONARIES, etc.); topic subdivisions limit the main subject further (RAILROADS—EMPLOYEES, RAILROADS—NARROW GAUGE, etc.). The subdivisions of subject headings are arranged according to a logic of their own. Arrangement within subdivisions is by main entry.

The point of this cursory glance at filing rules is to alert students to the importance of asking for assistance should they fail to find what they need in a card catalog. These conventions also offer a contrast to the computerized catalog, which is not alphabetically based and will usually provide more access points than its forerunner, the card catalog.

THE ONLINE CATALOG

Most computerized online public access catalogs, often referred to as OPACs or PACs, are developmental and created locally. Therefore, researchers cannot expect consistency from library to library. What they can expect is greater flexibility than the card method and comparative ease of use, although "user friendliness" will vary considerably from PAC to PAC. In some libraries, online catalogs provide access to databases beyond the individual library's holdings, for example, holdings in additional libraries or library systems or for nonbibliographic or commercially produced databases.

Online catalogs are usually searchable by any words, in any order, that appear in titles, series titles, or subject headings. Some may also be searched by publication type, such as book or periodical. Often, combinations of access points are possible, or particular searches may be narrowed. Logical connectors, known as Boolean logic, may be available.

PAC users appreciate the convenience of remaining in one location and simply entering their requests into the system, rather than moving about long rows of furniture and manipulating drawers and cards. Online searches often seem easier, faster, and more comprehensive, although they are not always. When an online system fails, users may refuse to revert to the card equivalent because it feels so cumbersome.

When a library's conversion from card to online catalog is prolonged, researchers may need to consult both sources for full holdings. Students must be clear about the coverage of each source. Because the computer is often perceived as omniscient and unfailing, it is also important that students be clear about what types of materials are included and excluded in the system. A common misconception is that a PAC indexes the contents of periodicals.

Although the particulars about teaching an online catalog must be determined by the individual library, it may be useful on one hand to start from a comparison to the card catalog. Students will then be introduced to general principles of access in a familiar context that provides a basis for comparison. (The comparative model is also useful for the discussion of commercial online database searching, which can be compared to searching a PAC.) On the other hand, an online catalog generally has more appeal to students. When it is introduced first, discussion of the computerized approach may generate more interest in the process of identifying books.

BIBLIOGRAPHIES

The term *bibliography* denotes both the study of books and a listing of materials: by country, language, publisher, time period, author, or subject. Published bibliographies are useful to the researcher to learn what is available in a field or on a particular subject, to identify sources that may not turn up through other means, to verify citations or acquire bibliographic information, for holdings information (i.e., locations), and to select or evaluate items.

Six types of bibliographies are noted here. Another type, the bibliographic guide, is discussed in chapter 6. Bibliographic guides go beyond a mere listing of items to provide additional information about a field or subject; they often focus on reference sources. Although the distinction between bibliographic guides and subject bibliographies is often unclear (or even unimportant), bibliographic guides are particularly useful for developing a search strategy because they often include a discussion of the field and relevant sources and may include supplementary lists of periodicals, organizations, etc.

National bibliographies. The catalogs of national libraries, such as the Library of Congress (although not an official national library), the British Library, and the Bibliotheque Nationale, are comprehensive because these libraries receive, by law, copies of all books registered for copyright in their country. The catalogs also list holdings published in other countries, making them universal in coverage. (A true national bibliography lists only items published in the particular country.)

The Library of Congress functions as the U.S. national library. The *National Union Catalog* (published by the Library of Congress with various cumulations and titles since 1898), *Books: Subjects* (based on the LC subject catalog and published since 1950), and the computer tapes LC MARC (Library of Congress Machine Readable Cataloging) and REMARC (Retrospective Machine Readable Cataloging) are used as the national bibliography of the United States, but they also include holdings published in other countries.

Trade bibliographies. Commercial publishers produce lists of books that are currently in print. Many foreign countries have an equivalent to the U.S. *Books in Print* (*BIP*), which is published by Bowker in parts for authors, titles, subjects, forthcoming, and paperbacks. *BIP* is available online and in compact disk.

The *Cumulative Book Index*, published by Wilson since 1898, lists books published worldwide in English during the time period covered (monthly with cumulations).

Retrospective bibliographies. In the United States and many foreign countries, historical bibliographies have been published to preserve records of bibliographical, social, cultural, and scientific development in print. A key retrospective bibliography for the United States is:

> Evans, Charles. *American Bibliography: A Chronological Dictionary of All Books, Pamphlets, and Periodical Publications Printed in the United States of America from the Genesis of Printing in 1639 Down to and Including the Year 1800.* Chicago: Printed for the author, 1903–1959. 14 vols.

Author bibliographies. Author bibliographies list works by or about an author.

Subject bibliographies. Subject bibliographies list works on a given topic. They may be complete or selected; the latter are often called reading lists or checklists.

The publisher G. K. Hall has made available, in book form, the catalogs of special collections in many libraries, including *The Harvard University Catalogue of the Peabody Museum Library*, which covers anthropology, and *The Stanford University Library Catalogs of the Hoover Institution on War, Revolution, and Peace.*

Author and subject bibliographies can be identified by browsing in the appropriate numerical section of the Z class; looking in the catalog under the author's last name or appropriate headings for a topic and the subdivision Bibliography; and consulting *Bibliographic Index*, bibliographic guides, and periodical indexes.

Bibliographies of bibliographies. An example of a subject listing of bibliographies is:

> *Bibliographic Index: A Cumulative Bibliography of Bibliographies.* New York: Wilson, 1938–   (semimonthly with annual cumulations). Includes bibliographies with fifty or more citations that were published separately or as parts of books, pamphlets, or periodicals.

Locating Books

In most libraries, books are arranged on shelves according to call numbers derived from a classification system. The call number serves as the book's address and is used to locate the book. Classification is the systematic arrangement of objects or ideas on the basis of some feature or features they have in common; classification serves to arrange like things together. Two different classification schemes are used nationally: the Library of Congress System and the Dewey Decimal System. The Library of Congress scheme is most likely to be used in an academic library.

Classification is fraught with difficulties. Most books are not simply focused on a single subject, and it is often difficult to determine a central or dominant theme. Researchers are sometimes surprised to find a particular book classified differently from what they expected or would prefer. One active and vocal library user feels personally offended that atheism is classified in religion. Most works on feminism continue to be classed in sociology, regardless of their perspective, because the early books were placed there as works addressing a social group.

Other recent and interdisciplinary subjects have outgrown their original placement and are strewn about the classification scheme. Psychology was early seen as most closely related to philosophy and classed in BF. As the field expanded, experimental works were placed in RC with medicine, physiological material was classed in QP, educational psychology was added to the LB class with education, and industrial psychology was placed in HF.

Books may be not only cross-disciplinary, but also pseudodisciplinary. While books on creationism have been classed with religion rather than biological evolution, revisionist versions of the Holocaust may be classed as history.

Donnelly describes another case:

> In the court and in academic inquiry [the *Protocols of the Elders of Zion*] has been proven a forgery that is based on a plagiarism. Surely such a fraudulent work alleging a secret conspiracy of Jews to dominate the entire world must be classified under "Imposture." Yet, the work can be found in a university collection under simple "Anti-Semitism" at DS145 in the European history section. No distinction is made in the system between scholarly books about anti-Semitism and works that are anti-Semitic.[1]

Despite the problems of classification, familiarity with classification schemes—especially with the classes covering a particular area of interest or academic major—does allow for browsing in the stacks, which will often produce serendipity, or "happy accidents." Of course, browsing cannot be relied upon alone, because all books will never be on the shelves at any one time. Also, it is important to remember that reference books and often rare books will be shelved as separate collections and that bibliographies are not necessarily shelved in the LC class for the subject covered, but in the Z class. However, card and online catalogs, characterized by inconsistencies and deficiencies, cannot be relied upon either. A thoughtful combination of both approaches will produce maximum results.

The Use and Evaluation of Books

Because libraries mean books to most undergraduates, students often begin research by looking for books, without considering what the source may offer for a particular topic. Although books are exceedingly diverse, a few generalizations indicate their role in research.

Most books are retrospective. It generally takes a long time to write a book and to get a book published. It also takes time for a library to acquire and process a book. By the time a library researcher has a book in hand, it is likely to be out of date, especially given the current acceleration of knowledge. Few or no books are likely to be available for current interest topics, although books may be useful for background information on such topics.

The importance of books varies among the disciplines. In the sciences, books are primarily archival, descriptive, and theoretical. Scientists rely on current journals for textual data and as a forum for communication. For humanists, however, books are both primary sources and an accepted vehicle for communication. In the social sciences, books serve both archival and contemporary functions.

Although book lengths differ considerably (many current paperbacks use wide margins, large type, and other means to appear longer), most books are extensive and in-depth. Undergraduate research time constraints usually preclude cover-to-cover reading of many books on a subject. Students who rely only on books for their research may discover few approaches to and perspectives on a topic and may feel overwhelmed by detail. However, books may be essential to establish a foundation or refer to when relevant information can be readily identified.

Books address all types of audiences. While the level of a periodical may be immediately discernible from the cover, a book may require a fuller investigation to determine its level. The references within a text may be an indication of the author's credibility: the researcher can note the extent to which the work is documented as well as the dates and nature of the sources cited. Since a single book may provide a considerable amount of information for a research project, it may also be worth the researcher's while to verify the author's reliability by consulting biographical sources or reading reviews of the book.

Researchers can learn techniques to quickly and efficiently overview books and extract relevant information. In fact, a book should be approached much like a new reference source (see chapter 2). The title page should be studied carefully, as well as the table of contents. Features, such as an index, notes, or bibliography, should be noted. The introduction or preface should be read, and the conclusion also. The researcher can peruse chapters or sections that are particularly relevant. Each chapter can also be overviewed by reading its introduction, scanning paragraphs and subheadings for main points, and reading its summary or conclusion.

The questions posed as the four levels of critical evaluation in chapter 10 make explicit the often unconscious process that a researcher engages in when scanning a text to become familiar with and assess it. In addition to evaluating individual books, researchers can assess the contribution of books in general to a particular research topic by asking the following questions:

> What kind of information do the books provide?
> What is missing from the books—certain perspectives, latest developments, bibliographies?
> How many books have been published on the subject?
> How accessible are books on the subject?
>> How descriptive are the subject headings for the topic?
>> Are books concentrated under a few or many headings?
>> How many books on the topic are available in the library?
>> Are most of the books shelved together or scattered under a variety of call numbers?
>> How many of the books are actually on the shelves?
> What contribution do books make to the research project?
> Are all points of view represented in the books?

In research, then, books are useful for in-depth, retrospective information. Their approach may be popular or scholarly, and the researcher must determine the author's credibility. Given their length, books are time-consuming to read and assimilate, but scanning techniques and critical evaluation enable the researcher to efficiently take advantage of this archetypal information format. The effective researcher will combine books with periodicals and other sources of information for a balanced approach.

Sample Learning Objectives

Concepts to understand:

> The value of developing a strategy and tactics to identify books.
> The nature, coverage, and use of the card catalog.
> The nature, coverage, and use of the online catalog.
> The types and uses of bibliographies.
> The functions and problems of classification.

The value and shortcomings of browsing to identify books.
The nature of books and their roles in research.
The importance of overviewing and evaluating books.

Skills to apply:

Developing a strategy and tactics for the book search.
Identifying books by author, title, and subject in a card catalog, online catalog, and bibliographies.
Locating books by call number and browsing in LC classes.
Overviewing and evaluating books.
Documenting and annotating books.

Sample In-Class Discussion Questions

1. What are the three basic approaches to finding materials in the card catalog?
2. What are the function and value of subject tracings?
3. What is the difference between word by word and letter by letter filing?
4. What should you do if you fail to find something listed in the card catalog?
5. What are the differences in access and coverage of the card catalog and the PAC?
6. How are bibliographies useful in research?
7. What are the differences between retrospective, national, and trade bibliographies?
8. How can author and subject bibliographies be identified?
9. What is classification?
10. How do the LC and Dewey systems differ?
11. What is the role of books in the research of the humanities, the sciences, the social sciences?
12. What is the nature of books?
13. How do you overview a book?
14. How do you determine the credibility of an author?

Sample In-Class Activities

1. Individually or in small groups, students are given a list of words to alphabetize word by word and letter by letter.

Sample lists:

Management by Objectives	Childers, Jane
The Mandarins	*A Child's History*
The Man Died	*Child Development*
Manacher, Glenda	*The Child, the Parent, and*
Man and Wildlife	*the State*
Mann, Thomas	*The Child*
Man into Space	*Child Study*
A Man Without Shoes	*Childbirth without Fear*
Man, Stephanie	*Childhood and Adolescence*
Manage Your Time	Child Welfare League
	Childs, Lois
	Child, Frances
	Children Who Hate
	Childe Harold's Pilgrimage
	Child Psychology

2. Individually or in small groups, students are given a list of call numbers to put in order.
   Sample list:

P	P	P	P	P	P	PA	P	QP
465	46	46	46	46	46.9	465	46	46
.R7	.R7	.R42	.R78	.R762	.R78	.R7	.R395	.B89

3. Students form small groups. Each group is given a topic and a relevant subject guidebook, subject bibliography, and subject volume of *Books in Print*. Group members look for books on their given topic in each source, compare the coverage of the three types of bibliographies, and list the differences. Each group reports back to the class at large.
4. Working from a one- or two-page outline of the LC classification system, as a class or in small groups, students decide where to classify some troublesome subject areas. Sample subjects:

   Atheism
   Feminist pedagogy
   Creationist theory
   Revisionist history of the Holocaust
   Computer-aided graphic design.

5. Given the results (photocopies of cards or computer printouts or lists of citations) of searches for the same topic in the card and online catalogs and working in small groups, students analyze the differences between the two access sources and report back to the class.

6. In small groups, students overview a book and select a chapter or section to critically evaluate (see the four levels of critical evaluation in chapter 10).

Sample Take-Home Exercises

1. Students develop a strategy for identifying books on a topic by determining what access sources and search modes to use, and what to look under in each mode. They describe the process and assess their results, noting how they proceeded when results were unexpected or unsatisfactory. They also assess the library's coverage of their topic.

2. For a given topic, students describe the differences in structure, access, and coverage of the online catalog, the card catalog, and *Books in Print*.

3. Students assess one book or chapter of a book by answering the questions in the four levels of critical evaluation and producing the results indicated.

4. Students identify books on a topic by looking in the PAC, card catalog, and bibliographies.

   A sample procedure might include:

   a. Before you begin your search for books on a subject, develop a search strategy. Decide which search modes to use in PAC and what to search for in each mode. Describe your strategy and the results, and assess the strategy.

   b. Look for older books in the card catalog and newer books in *Books in Print*. Comment on the quantity of cards you discover in the catalog and the relevance of titles. How do your findings compare to your expectations? Do LC subject headings provide adequate access? Compare this mode of access and the results to PAC and *BIP*.

   c. During your three searches, make bibliography cards for books which appear to be the most relevant. Locate two to four of the books and annotate the cards. Browse in the stacks for additional titles that sound useful and make more bib cards if you spot anything interesting.

d. Discuss the value of books as a source of information. Include the accessibility of such sources on your subject (subject headings, library holdings, availability on the shelves) as well as the nature of the information itself and what these sources contributed to your understanding of the subject.

Note and Suggested Reading

1. F. K. Donnelly, "Catalogue Wars and Classification Controversies," *Canadian Library Journal* 43:246 (Aug. 1986).

Chapter 10

Critical Evaluation

Given the overwhelming quantity of information and variety of perspectives in the learning society, critical evaluation is invaluable for transcending the limitations of egocentric or insular thinking and for seeking authority on the basis of demonstrated, verifiable expertise. Research is enhanced by awareness of the politics of language and information processing and the use of evaluation techniques.

The Challenge of the Learning Society

All experience, including the perception of information, is filtered through an individual's beliefs and attitudes, which have been constructed and reinforced since infancy. This frame of reference operates largely unconsciously and includes a variety of biases and prejudices. According to Richard Paul:

> We intellectually and affectively absorb, like plankton, common frames of reference from the social settings in which we live our lives. Our interests and purposes find a place within a socially absorbed picture of the world. We use that picture of the world to test the claims of contesting others. We imaginatively rehearse situations within portions of that picture. We rarely, however, describe that picture as a picture, as an image constructed by one social group as against that of another. It is difficult, therefore, to place that picture at arm's length, so to speak, and, for a time, suspend our acquiescence to it. That our thought is often disturbed and distorted by ethnocentric tendencies is rarely an abiding recognition. At best, it occurs in most people in fleeting glimpses, if we are to judge by the extent to which it is recognized explicitly in everyday thought.[1]

127

The communication of information is necessarily relative and therefore value-based. As Paul describes above, it is difficult enough to acknowledge, let alone separate from, one's world view. This frame of reference, then, becomes the context for expression as well as values. As noted in chapter 1, the publication of information does not ensure that it is reliable, and, in fact, much of what constitutes the information explosion is deliberately biased or commercially motivated. Even the credibility of science as a neutral, objective approach is increasingly questioned. As the physicist Fritjof Capra comments:

> The patterns scientists observe in nature are intimately connected with the patterns of their minds—with their concepts, thoughts and values. Hence, the scientific results they obtain and the technological applications they investigate will be conditioned by their frame of mind.[2]

The central challenge of the learning society is to break through the constraints of predispositions or prejudices and to stretch beyond acquiescence to alleged authority. This is accomplished, first, by recognizing personal bias and setting it aside in order to enter into and examine other perspectives with deferred judgment (a component of creative problem solving). Second, it is necessary to systematically analyze and assess information. Beyond the packaging of information and credentials of the communicator, students can identify internal evidence of accuracy, logic, appropriateness, and ultimate validity through critical evaluation.

The Politics of Selection and Language

Bias is insidious because it is universal, and few individuals can readily articulate their own prejudices. An excellent analysis of the forces that give rise to bias and prejudice and how their effects can be reduced is offered by Charles West. He diagrams the process by which individuals select information from all the stimuli available in the environment. Humans can sense only certain types of stimuli, and any individual can perceive only a limited number of stimuli at any one moment. Further selection is consciously and unconsciously based on the perceiver's knowledge, emotions, biases, and social context. These factors constitute the perceiver's frame of reference, which includes concepts, structures, affect, needs, values, and interests. Individuals tend to select that information that is in keeping with their interests, attitudes, and values.

West also demonstrates how these same factors influence science.

Scientists are circumscribed not only by their personal frames of reference but also by the methodology and world view of the scientific community which trains and supports them and evaluates their work.[3] Thomas Kuhn describes the communal scientific frame of reference as a paradigm that enforces limitations: "In science...novelty emerges only with difficulty, manifested by resistance, against a background provided by expectation."[4]

Elliot Eisner describes the politics of method:

> Neither technique nor technology, whether technology of a physical type or technology of mind, is epistemologically neutral. The categories we are taught, the sources of evidence that we believe count, the language that we learn to use govern our world-views. How we come to see the world, what we think it means, and eventually what we believe we can do about that world are intimately related to the technologies of mind we have acquired. There is no such thing as a value-neutral approach to the world; language itself, whether the language of the arts or the sciences, is value-laden.[5]

The value-added impact of language is unequivocally demonstrated when words like "whore," "prick," "nigger," and "kike" are recited evenly and calmly in the classroom. Emotional responses occur immediately, despite the controlled utterance. The emotional charge in a less neutral context is undeniable. Although these are obvious examples, there is the potential for reaction to many words that carry negative connotations. Women and members of racial and ethnic groups, in particular, may be highly sensitive to words that convey a disregard for equity because language reinforces the social structure. Feminists and others continue to maintain, as the black movement asserted in the 1960s, that language must be changed in order to change society.

These issues become critical in library research because the search for information is conducted with words. Acknowledging the political nature of language, the researcher will recognize the importance of vocabulary control and the values that are implicit in the indexing vocabularies of access sources. Matching a personal vocabulary with established vocabularies is one of the challenges of effective research (see chapter 8).

Challenging and Accepting Information

Two approaches are useful for experiencing one's own bias and the point of view embedded in a piece of literature: methodologically challenging and accepting. West encourages a healthy skepticism with his four guidelines for critical evaluation. He suggests that every communication be viewed as propaganda. He urges readers and listeners to analyze the goals or intentions of the communicator, and to determine the writer's or speaker's frame of reference. Lastly, West encourages critical evaluators to:

> Be aware of the fact that the writer or speaker is not providing all relevant data on the issue. The writer has selected certain data or ideas over others to communicate. That data and those ideas were selected which were consistent with his intentions.[6]

Peter Elbow offers a counterpoint to this approach:

> We need [methodological doubt,] the systematic, disciplined, and conscious attempt to criticize everything no matter how compelling it might seem—to find flaws or contradictions we might otherwise miss. But thinking is not trustworthy unless it also includes methodological belief: the equally systematic, disciplined, and conscious attempt to *believe* everything no matter how unlikely or repellent it might seem—to find virtues or strengths we might otherwise miss. Both processes derive their power from the very fact that they are methodological: artificial, systematic, and disciplined uses of the mind. As methods, they help us see what we would miss if we only used our minds naturally or spontaneously.[7]

Alternately challenging and accepting information, students explore perspectives from outside their subjectivity by systematically questioning or believing everything in a piece of literature. It is challenging to listen openly to a point of view with which one disagrees, and it is equally challenging to critically question a stance with which one agrees. These approaches provide structures for entering into alternative perspectives. Such forced attitudes offer the student an opportunity to systematically analyze a point of view. In the process, students are likely to discover a deeper understanding of their own perspective. As noted in the anthology of readings for critical thinking, *Censorship: Opposing Viewpoints*:

> To have a good grasp of one's own viewpoint, it is necessary to understand the arguments of those with whom one disagrees. It can be said that those who do not completely understand their adversary's point of view do not fully understand their own.[8]

Critical Evaluation of Library Sources

In addition to methodologically determining biases, students can also systematically analyze and assess information. Chapter 2 presents procedures for studying and evaluating reference sources. Those procedures are also applicable to sources of information; in addition, a more thorough approach to the evaluation of subject content is needed. Students are often convinced that they are not capable of analyzing an expert. The following process for critical evaluation demonstrates that it is the systematic application of reasoning skills, not merely subject knowledge, that is the basis of evaluation. The process encourages students, as Stephen Brookfield suggests, to:

> Not take for granted the universal truth of some statement, policy, or justification simply because of the authority ascribed to the source of this supposed truth. . . . [but to] call into question the belief that simply because some idea or social structure has existed unchanged for a period of time, it therefore must be (a) right and (b) the best possible arrangement.[9]

Critical evaluation of library materials is progressive, involving four levels of examination, as shown in figure 14. The student first becomes familiar with the piece of literature to determine if it is relevant. The title page and preface or introduction are read to ascertain the intent and scope of the work, and the student overviews the table of contents or subheads and any special features. The approach and conclusion are noted. The researcher poses questions to be answered by the source and then peruses it to determine whether the questions are addressed. If the item appears useful, the student can sketch a quick outline or note particularly relevant sections.

At the second level, the student seeks to understand the piece and identify main points. Short pieces are read completely; longer works are scanned and key selections read. While scanning and reading, the student makes lists of key terms and conclusions. The work should be briefly summarized or abstracted at this point.

On the analyzing level, the student looks at how the data and conclusions are presented and examines the style and structure, looking for patterns, logical connections, consistency, and bias. At this point, the researcher should be actively responding to the piece, but deferring final judgment until the analysis is complete.

Finally, the critical evaluator reaches the level of assessing the overall quality and contribution of the piece based on the internal validity

1st Level—Becoming Familiar with a Piece of Literature

QUESTIONS
Why Should I Read This Piece of Literature?

What is the full title and year of publication?	Who are the author(s) and publisher?	What is included in the table of contents or headings?	Are there any features, such as an index, bibliography, glossary, illustrations, etc.?	What are the intention and scope as indicated by an introduction?
Are the language and approach suitable to my level?	What questions would I like this work to answer?	Does it appear to address my questions?	Is the conclusion relevant to my interest?	

Results: 1. A list of questions.
2. An overview (outline or list) of areas covered.

2nd Level: Understanding a Piece of Literature

QUESTIONS
What Does This Piece of Literature Convey?

What is the author's thesis?	What are the key concepts?	What are the main points?	What is the methodology?	What are the findings and conclusions?

Results: 1. Lists of key terms, concepts, data, conclusions.
2. A *summary* or *abstract* of the piece.

3rd Level—Analyzing a Piece of Literature

QUESTIONS
How Are the Data Presented? Do the Conclusions Follow?

| What are the author's frame of reference and intentions? | What biases are evident? | Is the language clear and appropriate? Is the style appropriate? | Does the organizational structure promote understanding of the information? | Are transitions clear? Is the piece coherent? |

| Are the connections logical? | What patterns of thought emerge? | Are sources current and reliable? | Do conclusions follow from the data? | Is there consistency within the piece and with other materials? |

Results: Responses to (1) the author's stand, (2) the approach, (3) the style, (4) the results.

4th Level: Assessing a Piece of Literature

QUESTIONS
What Is the Quality of This Piece of Literature?

| What are your own biases on this subject and your expectations for this work? | Did the author fulfill her or his goals? | How does it feel to challenge points in this work? | How does it feel to accept points in this work? | Does the piece make a contribution to the literature? |

| Does the piece make a contribution to your research? |

Results: An *evaluative statement* about the work and its usefulness to the research (i.e., an annotation).

Figure 14. Critical evaluation

of the work, its general usefulness, and its value to the student's research. Students must be clear about their own expectations and biases in order to assess objectively as well as subjectively. As research progresses, it should become easier to judge an author's contribution to the literature in a comparative context.

At the completion of this process, the researcher annotates the bibliography card for the item with a brief description or summary and an evaluative comment, noting especially what contribution the work makes to the research.

The list of questions in figure 14 attempts to make explicit the process applied intuitively by effective evaluators. The procedure may seem obvious and forced to students who use it intuitively, and slow and laborious to students who resist the process. With practice, however, the procedure becomes internalized. A parallel to this process is the learning of most procedural skills (such as starting up a car or computer). When the procedure is first presented as a rigid sequence of discrete steps, performing it feels awkward and painstaking. With practice, however, the steps soon merge into a smooth, rapid flow.

As a supplement to their own assessment of an item, researchers may also wish to use library sources to determine an author's background or identify published reviews or literary criticism. Chapter 2 discusses reference sources for biographical information and reviews.

The rewards of critical evaluation include opening to new viewpoints and a deeper understanding of one's own perspective as well as more efficient and effective use of information sources. Despite the quantity and ubiquity of information in the learning society, researchers can determine what is relevant and appropriate using systematic criteria.

Sample Learning Objectives

Concepts to understand:

> All experience and information as filtered through frames of reference.
> Words as value-laden and language as political.

Skills to apply:

> Challenging all information.
> Methodologically believing all aspects of a perspective.
> Critically evaluating library sources.

Sample Class Discussion Questions

1. What is a frame of reference, and how is it developed and maintained?
2. What is objectivity? Is science objective?
3. Can we know reality or only our subjective perception of reality?
4. How do you feel when you hear words that are racist and sexist slurs? What other kinds of words may be emotionally charged for a particular individual?
5. Why can all communication be viewed as propaganda?
6. How can you determine an author's frame of reference?
7. How can you get inside another person's perspective?
8. How do you evaluate the information you read?
9. How do you overview or scan library materials?
10. What is an annotation?
11. How can you learn about an author's background?
12. How can you locate reviews?

Sample In-Class Activities

1. Students respond to a newspaper article or editorial on a current, controversial topic. Students identify the biases implicit in their reactions.
2. Students debate whether all words should be officially modified to be gender-free.
3. Students take sides on a controversial issue (such as abortion, pornography, or censorship). In small groups or to the class, students argue for the side they actually oppose. The audience evaluates the believability of their stance.
4. Given photocopies of a short article, students as a class address the questions listed under "Critical Evaluation of Library Sources."
5. In small groups provided with a book or periodical article, students address the questions listed under "Critical Evaluation of Library Sources."

Sample Take-Home Exercises

1. Students apply the procedure for critically evaluating library sources to a book or article (on their topic).

2. Students find an article that supports their point of view on a subject. They determine the author's frame of reference and systematically challenge every major point made in the article.

Notes and Suggested Reading

1. Richard W. Paul, "Critical Thinking and the Critical Person," in *Thinking: The Second International Conference*, eds. D. N. Perkins, Jack Lochhead, and John Bishop (Hillsdale, N.J.: Erlbaum, 1987), p. 386.

2. Fritjof Capra, *The Tao of Physics: An Exploration of the Parallels between Modern Physics and Eastern Mysticism*, 2nd ed., rev. and updated (Boston: Shambhala, 1985), p. 9.

3. Charles K. West, *The Social and Psychological Distortion of Information* (Chicago: Nelson-Hall, 1981).

4. Thomas S. Kuhn, *The Structure of Scientific Revolutions*, 2nd ed. enl., Foundations of the Unity of Science, vol. II, no. 2 (Chicago: Univ. of Chicago Pr., 1975), p. 64.

5. Elliot W. Eisner, "The Primacy of Experience and the Politics of Method," *Educational Researcher* 17:19 (June–July 1988).

6. West, *The Social and Psychological Distortion of Information*, pp. 89–90.

7. Peter Elbow, *Embracing Contraries: Explorations in Learning and Teaching* (New York: Oxford Univ. Pr., 1986), pp. 257–258.

8. David L. Bender, "Why Consider Opposing Viewpoints?" in *Censorship: Opposing Viewpoints*, ed. Terry O'Neill, Opposing Viewpoints Series (St. Paul, Minn.: Greenhaven, 1985), p. 9.

9. Stephen D. Brookfield, *Developing Critical Thinkers: Challenging Adults to Explore Alternative Ways of Thinking and Acting* (San Francisco: Jossey-Bass, 1987), p. 21.

Chapter 11

Newspapers

A presupposition of our information and learning society is that it is a free society with a free flow of information. Freedom of the press has been protected as a safeguard of that principle. However, as the most prevalent and frequently used sources of information in this society, the news media are far too likely to be viewed indiscriminately and relied upon as principal sources. Students should understand the role of newspapers in both society and research.

A variety of sources are available for identifying newspapers and newspaper articles on a subject. Newspapers have long been preserved on microfilm and, increasingly, newspaper indexes are available in computerized formats. The study of newspapers can be enlivened by a focus on First Amendment issues.

The Nature and Use of Newspapers

Democracy is participatory government, and as such it is predicated upon the free flow of information and ideas. The mass media are a primary channel of this flow. Newspapers provide an example of some of the best and worst aspects of the popular media. They are inexpensive, readily available, current, and diverse in content and style. Concurrently, they are commercially motivated, popularly oriented, and often suspect in terms of accuracy, objectivity, and fairness.

Newspapers can be used to distinguish between primary and secondary material as well as between popular and scholarly sources.

This chapter is based on the author's article, "Newspapers in Bibliographic Instruction," *Colorado Libraries* 13:22–24 (March 1987).

Firsthand accounts, as opposed to editorials, demonstrate the distinction between primary and secondary material. In contrast to newspaper articles, scholarly periodical articles and monographs require significant periods of time for development and publication, typically emanate from a particular discipline, and include published sources as documentation. As a popular source, newspaper articles require careful evaluation for research applications. They are useful for firsthand accounts, human interest aspects, contemporary or opposing viewpoints, and background information, but the immediate and transitory nature of newspaper articles nevertheless affects their validity.

Access

For most research purposes, students will need to identify newspaper articles on a particular subject or event. Browsing to locate information in newspapers may be necessary for current events or when no index is available. While newspaper indexes are generally a more efficient approach for locating information, the time lag for print indexes may render them useless for very current subjects; microfilm, CD-ROM, and online indexes are more up to date. Students may also need to identify newspapers published in a particular geographic location; a variety of directories serve this purpose. To locate newspapers, students must consult in-house serials listings, local newspaper lists, or national holdings lists for newspapers on microfilm.

Students are likely to assume that all newspapers are indexed, but only a minimal number of newspapers are commercially indexed, and most newspaper indexes have been available for only a decade or two. The indexes to the *New York Times* and the London *Times* are examples of access sources that span the century and can be used in historical research to identify contemporary material, both primary and secondary. These indexes are also useful for pinpointing dates to facilitate browsing in papers that are not indexed. The *New York Times Index* (1851–) can be used not only as an index to that newspaper, but also for abstracts of the news, and to identify book, film, and play reviews, obituaries, and brief biographical information.

Most newspaper indexes cover a single paper, but the *National Newspaper Index* (on microfilm and online) and *NewsBank* (in printed index and CD-ROM) include several titles. Users should note which titles are covered. Even in single title newspaper indexes, it is important to note which regional editions are covered when the paper is distributed nationally. As most newspaper indexes do not list every item in the newspaper, students should read introductory material to determine selection criteria.

Students should also deliberately select the particular issues of an index to search. Beginning with the time period most likely to cover the topic, they should look forwards or backwards in time as appropriate, noting the cumulation pattern of the index. Some newspaper indexes are in one alphabetical sequence, while the Bell and Howell indexes for the *Christian Science Monitor*, *Los Angeles Times*, and *Denver Post*, for example, list personal names and subjects separately.

The citations in newspaper indexes might be compared to periodical index citations. Briefer bibliographic information is required to identify newspaper articles. The descriptive notes in newspaper indexes are more useful than article titles, but less informative than a true abstract. The *New York Times Index*, however, claims that it "can be used by itself for a basic chronological overview of the news."

Periodical directories and holdings lists are also useful for accessing newspapers. Directories, to find out what newspapers are published in a given geographical area, include the *Gale Directory of Publications*, *Editor and Publisher International Yearbook*, and *Working Press of the Nation* (Volume 1: Newspaper Directory). A key national holdings list is *Newspapers in Microform* (published by the Library of Congress, 1984).

News Digests

News digests summarize the news and are a quick source of information. They are an alternative to newspaper indexes or backfiles of newspapers (often on microfilm) when a researcher needs merely a brief summary of a news event. They can also provide a starting point in a broader search. News digests are typically issued weekly, in looseleaf form, to be added to a binder in chronological order; a cumulating subject index is also issued. Examples of news digests include the New York publication *Facts On File* and the London-based *Keesing's Contemporary Archives*, as well as English language news digests for other countries, such as *Africa Diary*, *Asian Recorder*, *Current Digest of the Soviet Press*, and *Latin America Weekly Report*.

First Amendment Issues

A free press has always been considered essential in our free society. The first constitutional amendment states that "Congress shall make no law...abridging the freedom of speech, or of the press...." For almost 200 years since, the balance between freedom, responsibility, and government regulation has been precarious.[1] Freedom of the press can be discussed in terms of censorship, access to government information, and protection of sources. Responsibility of the press can be addressed with discussion of libel, invasion of privacy, and truth in reporting.

An enduring controversy is censorship or prior restraint. The press was specifically protected from censorship with the 1931 Supreme Court decision in *Near vs. Minnesota*:

> The fact that the liberty of the press may be abused by miscreant purveyors of scandal does not make any the less necessary the immunity of the press from previous restraint in dealing with official misconduct. Subsequent punishment for such abuses as may exist is the appropriate remedy consistent with constitutional privilege.[2]

This decision specified three areas of exception: public decency, incitement to violence, and national security during war. The "Pentagon Papers" case in 1971 (New York Times *vs. United States*, and *United States vs.* Washington Post) was a dramatic government test of the national security exemption to prior restraint of the press. A restraining order halted for fifteen days publication by the *New York Times* and the *Washington Post* of Daniel Ellsberg's secret history of the Vietnam conflict. The Supreme Court lifted the order because the government had not met its burden of proof to show justification. The separate opinions submitted by the nine justices, however, are not considered an overwhelming mandate against censorship.

The increasing classification of government documents to ensure secrecy is of growing concern. A number of Reagan administration policies served to restrict access to government information, including limitations to the Freedom of Information Act (1966). Conflict between the government and the press may also occur when press coverage jeopardizes a fair trial or when a journalist refuses to reveal a confidential source. Thus, freedom of the press, though essential for participatory government and an information and learning society, is not without controversial regulation.

While prior restraint of the press is restricted, libel and privacy laws offer subsequent recourse to individual citizens who believe they have been defamed or invaded by the press. Intended to encourage "responsibility" of the press, such laws can have an impact upon freedom of the press. According to a prominent communications lawyer:

Publishers and broadcasters of all kinds are now coming to realize that the cost of defending libel and privacy suits—and the
uncertainty of result because of unclear guidelines—adds another link of self-censorship to the chain which can eventually
strangle free expression through governmental intimidation
rather than action.[3]

Truth in reporting is another issue related to responsibility of the
press. Whether the mission of journalism is the accurate presentation
of facts or the selling of stories is a question debated within and without the field. A senior writer for *Time* concludes that: "A culture that
would rely on the news for truth...would have lost the qualities of
mind that make the news worth knowing."[4] Clearly, to be used effectively, especially in research, newspapers must be approached from
within a framework of critical thinking.

Sample Learning Objectives

Concepts to understand:

The role of newspapers in society and in research.
Newspapers as a popular source in contrast to scholarly sources.
The nature and functions of newspaper indexes, directories, hold-
ings lists, and news digests.
Freedom and responsibilities of the press.

Skills to apply:

Using newspaper indexes to identify articles on a particular subject.
Using newspaper directories to identify newspapers published in
particular geographic locations.
Locating and documenting newspaper articles.
Applying the guidelines of critical evaluation to assess newspaper
articles.

Sample Class Discussion Questions

1. What functions do newspapers serve for the individual, soci-
    ety, and research?
2. Why is it important to critically evaluate newspaper articles?

3. What are some problems in accessing newspapers?
4. What are some uses of the *New York Times Index*?
5. How can you identify newspapers published in a particular geographic location?
6. What are news digests? How might they be used in research?
7. Should prior restraint protections to the freedom of the press include secret military maneuvers?
8. Should more or less government information be classified and thereby less available to reporters?
9. Should there be any restrictions to media coverage of trials?
10. Should confidentiality of newspaper reporter sources be protected?
11. Do libel laws inhibit the free press or promote responsibility of the press?
12. What are the ethical responsibilities of journalists?

Sample In-Class Activities

1. Working in small groups, half of the groups discuss the value of newspapers, while the other half discuss problems with newspapers. Each group summarizes its discussion for the class at large.
2. In small groups, students note the coverage, arrangement, and access of periodical directories, and they identify newspapers published in given geographic locations. Each group reports back to the class at large.
3. In small groups, students evaluate a newspaper article and editorial on the same subject, according to the guidelines for critical evaluation (see chapter 10).
4. Students select a controversial aspect of freedom of the press and debate alternative perspectives.

Sample Take-Home Exercise

Use the *National Newspaper Index* (on microfilm), the *New York Times Index*, and one other newspaper index to identify articles on a topic. Use a style manual to cite at least six articles.

Locate at least four articles on your topic from at least two different newspapers. At least one of your articles should be an editorial, and ideally you will find one editorial and one news article from each newspaper.

Apply the critical evaluation questions to a news article and an editorial.

In a brief essay, answer the following questions (not necessarily in this order). Be sure to cite the articles you are addressing in your essay.

Did the indexes provide adequate access?

If you browsed in newspapers for articles, how effective or frustrating was it?

What did you learn about your topic?

Compare the editorials and the news articles, addressing the extent of the bias in each.

Compare the coverage of your topic by the different newspapers.

Do you think newspaper articles made a good starting point for your research of this topic? Why or why not?

Notes and Suggested Reading

1. Thomas Eveslage, *The First Amendment: Free Speech and a Free Press: A Curriculum Guide for High School Teachers* (Philadelphia: Thomas Eveslage, 1985), p. 11.

2. Thomas L. Tedford, *Freedom of Speech in the United States* (Carbondale: Southern Illinois Univ. Pr., 1985), pp. 328–329.

3. Alan U. Schwartz, "Using the Courts to Muzzle the Press," in *The First Freedom Today: Critical Issues Relating to Censorship and to Intellectual Freedom*, eds. Robert B. Downs and Ralph E. McCoy (Chicago: American Library Assn., 1984), p. 282.

4. Roger Rosenblatt, "Journalism and the Larger Truth," in *Believing the News*, ed. Don Fry (St. Petersburg, Fla.: Poynter Institute for Media Studies, 1985), p. 237.

Chapter 12

Accessing and Evaluating
the Periodical Literature

An appealing metaphor for the periodical literature is conversation.
As Bechtel maintains:

> The primary task, then, of the academic library is to introduce
> students to the world of scholarly dialogue that spans both space
> and time and to provide students with the knowledge and skills
> they need to tap into conversations on an infinite variety of top-
> ics and to participate in the critical inquiry and debate on those
> issues.[1]

According to the typical bifurcation of the literature, popular periodicals speak to the community at large and scholarly periodicals
speak to specialists in a field.[2] A middle category of periodicals can be
identified that addresses both specialized and general audiences, i.e.,
the subject or professional magazine. Periodical articles are important
in research because they are concise and current (or contemporaneous
to an event), they often include references to additional sources of information, and they may offer viewpoints or information that never
appears in books.

Periodicals in a particular subject or geographic area can be identified by using periodical directories. Periodical articles on a subject or
by an author can be identified by consulting a variety of print, microform, and computer-based indexes. Procedures for locating periodicals are specific to individual libraries. The process of critical
evaluation is the student's entree to participation in the conversations
of authors.

Popular, Subject, and Scholarly Periodicals

Before approaching the periodical literature, students should know the terminology of serial publication. A *serial* is a publication issued in successive parts, usually at regular intervals (e.g., weekly, monthly, quarterly, annually), and intended to be continued indefinitely. Magazines, journals, proceedings, yearbooks, and indexes are all serials. *Periodical* is a generic term for both *magazines* (commercial publications intended for a general, popular audience) and *journals* (specialized, scholarly publications typically published by an institution, professional association, or learned society). *Subject* or *professional magazines* fall somewhere in between magazines and journals, with articles written by experts but intended less to advance the field than to report on developments of interest to an educated audience. Some examples are: *Anthropology Today*, *Hispanic Times*, *Smithsonian*, *Scientific American*. Sensational periodicals, such as *The National Enquirer* and the *Weekly World News*, constitute another category so obviously irrelevant to library research it will not be addressed here.

Undergraduate students will be familiar with popular newsstand magazines, such as *Time*, *Newsweek*, *Ms.*, and *Sports Illustrated*. Most students will know of some subject and professional magazines. Few undergraduates, however, will have ever seen or used a scholarly journal. An understanding of the differences between the types of periodicals is essential in library research.

Popular and scholarly publications look different. Popular magazines are more colorful with flashier covers intended to entice a reader. They have many illustrations and photographs, and the paper may even be glossier. Subject and professional magazines are similar in appearance to popular periodicals. Scholarly publications are drabber and less appealing in appearance. Their covers are typically of a single subdued color, featuring the journal title and selected article titles or the entire table of contents. The contents are predominantly text, with few or no advertisements. The attractive appearance of magazines is a deliberate attempt to catch the attention of potential buyers at newsstands and grocery checkouts. Scholarly journals are not widely available and not intended for the occasional buyer but rather for the continuous individual or institutional subscriber.

Titles are different also. Popular magazine titles are largely general or aimed at a special interest group; scholarly journal titles are typically more focused and addressed to very special interest groups. Scholarly journal titles often include words like "journal," "review," "annals." Titles of scholarly articles tend to be rather long and precise, whereas popular article titles are catchier or more generally descriptive.

The intended audiences are also quite distinct. Popular magazines, as evidenced by their appearance, coverage, and a typically low reading level, are intended for the general public. Readers are not assumed to have extensive prior knowledge of a subject. Scholarly journals are intended for students and practitioners of a particular discipline, as indicated by the serious tone, specialized language, and their dissemination mainly to libraries and other subscribers, who are likely to be members of the publishing association. Subject and professional magazines may be intended for both an interested audience as well as a specialized audience.

Popular and scholarly authors are different. The authors of popular articles may not be identified at all. They may be staff writers, paid to produce articles on subjects in which they have limited or no background other than the fact that they write about them. Scholarly authors are practitioners and teachers of their fields. They are often employed in higher education, and their affiliation is usually indicated with the article or in a list of contributors. They are probably not directly imbursed for the article; career promotion, salary increase, or tenure may hinge on publication. Scholarly authors, for the most part, write to communicate with their colleagues and to advance the knowledge of their discipline. They may also contribute to subject and professional magazines in order to disseminate information about their field to a wider audience.

Freides distinguishes between the social commentator and the social scientist. The former addresses the public regarding matters of immediate social concern, often with the intent to persuade. While the social scientist may focus on the same issues, the intent is to study an issue from a trained perspective, applying standardized procedures, in order to contribute to the knowledge base of the field. As Freides notes:

> The scientist aims to influence the other scholars working in his speciality, rather than the public at large, and what he seeks to persuade them of is not the fairness or righteousness of his views or the wisdom of the course he advocates, but the usefulness of his observations and explanations as a way to account for what goes on.[3]

Scholarly journals often have editorial or advisory boards. Instructions for submitting articles may appear in every issue or annually. Articles are usually "refereed"—reviewed by the author's peers to determine the article's acceptability. Authors may be asked to edit or revise before submissions are accepted. Given the current "publish or perish" syndrome in higher education, many articles are delayed or not accepted simply because of space shortage. Most popular articles are reports, digests, or persuasive pieces, while most scholarly articles are research-based. Popular articles report events, the author's opinion, or simplified versions (sometimes overly simplified) of the findings of others. They rarely include citations to publications, although they frequently incorporate quotes, from both so-called experts and individuals of interest, to add color. Subject and professional periodical articles report scholarly findings to an interested, educated audience and may or may not include citations. Generally, scholarly articles both review the previous literature and report original research or experimentation, adding to the literature of the field. The extensive footnotes and bibliographies in scholarly articles provide the researcher with a selected list of references to additional sources of information on the topic.

Because they are specialized, technical, and jargon-laden, scholarly articles are more difficult to read. Undergraduates will probably need a subject dictionary to help interpret them, but there is value in consulting the original literature rather than a nonexpert's watered-down and possibly biased version. Even without any background in a subject, undergraduates can systematically work through scholarly articles by applying the four levels of critical evaluation.

Often, scholarly articles are preceded by an abstract or summary of the article, which the student can use to quickly determine whether the article is relevant or not and as an introduction or guide to the article. Some abstracting indexes include author or journal abstracts; other index publishers develop their own abstracts.

Each type of literature has a function and value in research. Popular articles often make a good point of entry for research. They can provide a basic introduction to a topic, an overview that may suggest possible approaches to the subject, divergent points of view, and perhaps some color. The college-level researcher will go on to collect scholarly articles that offer more focused, in-depth, original, research-based information. Subject or professional magazines may serve both sets of functions and are particularly useful for research in scientific and technical areas in which the scholarly materials may be too specialized for undergraduates. They offer the authority of experts without the complexity of original research accounts.

Identifying Periodicals

Directories, such as the following, are useful to find out what periodicals are being published in a subject or geographical area.

Gale Directory of Publications: An Annual Guide to Newspapers, Magazines, Journals, and Related Publications. 120th ed. Detroit, Mich.: Gale, 1988. Lists more than 25,000 publications in the United States, Puerto Rico, the Virgin Islands, Canada, the Bahamas, Bermuda, Panama, and the Philippines. Better for newspapers than periodicals.

The International Directory of Little Magazines and Small Presses. Len Fulton, ed. 23rd ed. Paradise, Calif.: Dustbooks, 1987. Lists over 4,000 publications in paragraph-length entries.

The Serials Directory: An International Reference Book. Premier edition. Birmingham, Ala.: Ebsco, 1986. Lists more than 113,000 serial titles.

The Standard Periodical Directory: The Largest Authoritative Guide to United States and Canadian Periodicals. 11th ed. New York: Oxbridge Communications, 1988. Lists over 60,000 periodicals, classified in 239 subject categories. Includes consumer magazines; trade journals; newsletters; government publications; house organs; directories, transactions and proceedings of scientific societies; yearbooks; museum, religious, ethnic, literary, and social group publications.

Ulrich's International Periodicals Directory 1988–89. 27th ed. New York: Bowker, 1988. Lists more than 108,000 periodicals of all kinds from all over the world in 554 subject areas. Includes a subheading "Abstracting, Bibliographies, Statistics" for each major subject group.

Identifying Periodical Indexes

Periodical indexes typically list the articles in specified publications by subject and by author. Some indexes list not only articles, but also other types of publications, such as books, dissertations, conference proceedings, pamphlets, and government documents. Each item is described in a citation that provides the information necessary to locate it, including author, title, journal title, volume, pages, and date. Some periodical indexes include a summary or abstract of the article as well.

Just as there are both general and subject encyclopedias, dictionaries, and guidebooks, there are also general and subject indexes. General indexes, such as the *Readers' Guide to Periodical Literature*, the *Magazine Index* (on microfilm), and *InfoTrac* (on videodisk), provide access to popular and subject and professional magazines. Subject indexes, available for most disciplines, provide access primarily to scholarly journals.

There are several ways to identify abstracting and indexing tools for a given topic or discipline. The researcher can consult a general or subject guidebook or a listing of indexing publications, especially the Gale *Abstracting and Indexing Services Directory* (1982–   ), which includes print and nonprint publications. Many directories of online indexes are also available. However, students are well advised to always consult with a reference librarian to determine the available and most relevant indexes for a subject. Because so many indexes are currently published, index holdings will vary from library to library, and the location and arrangement of indexes in a given library or library system may not be apparent. A librarian can also indicate whether computer-based indexes are available as well as controlled vocabularies for particular indexes.

When identifying indexes, it is important to consider, in general and in particular, what is included and excluded. Well over 100,000 periodicals are currently published worldwide, and no single index can provide access to all of them. Undergraduates may assume that the *Readers' Guide* is the only index and that it covers all periodicals; the quantity and variety of subject indexes will be a revelation to them. It is important to stress further that even a subject index will not include all the journals of that field; most fields, in fact, support several indexes.

Index publishing is a commercial enterprise. Indexes cover those publications that are most widely read, referred to, established, and readily accessible. Publications out of the mainstream are less likely to be included because they emanate from emerging fields of study, represent special interests, are considered peripheral by the traditional academy, or are not published by the recognized commercial publishers. The interests of women, racial and ethnic minorities, radical politics, and homosexuals often fall into this category.

Research in nonmainstream areas, then, may require extra effort to identify and access relevant materials. Fortunately, there are a few indexes that address this need:

Access: The Supplementary Index to Periodicals. 1975– . Evanston, Ill.: Burke.
Alternative Press Index: An Index to Alternative and Radical Publications. 1969/70– . Baltimore, Md.: Alternative Press Center.
Index to Black Periodicals. 1950–59– . Boston, Mass.: Hall.
Left Index. 1982– . Santa Cruz, Calif.: Left Index.
Lesbian Periodicals Index. Clare Potter, comp. and ed. Tallahassee, Fla.: Naiad, 1986.
Women Studies Abstracts. 1972– . Rush, N.Y.: Rush.

Types of Indexes

Periodical indexes are available in several types and formats. In addition to indexing publications, such as the titles published by Wilson that list citations under subject headings and authors, there are also abstracting publications and citation indexes. All of these types are available in print, CD-ROM, and online. Just as students typically prefer online to card catalogs, they also readily embrace computer-based indexes. The advantages and approaches to online and CD-ROM indexes are discussed in chapter 13. The uses of print abstracting and citation indexes are described here.

In print abstracting indexes, citations are typically arranged under broad subject categories rather than under specific subject headings. This arrangement means that looking for citations is a two-step process. The researcher can use the table of contents to locate a topic within one of the subject categories and then browse in that section of the abstracts looking for relevant articles, or the researcher can look for a specific topic in the subject index and then locate the particular abstract numbers that are listed there. The summaries then make it easy for the researcher to pick out the most useful articles. The researcher should note the cumulation of indexes in abstracting publications.

Citation indexes, as Bechtel notes,

> Provide users with access to the contributions of all the participants in a particular discussion through the list of footnotes found in a book or article and through the list of articles and books that subsequently cite the central work.[4]

Citation indexes also provide access through keywords in titles. Citation indexes are available for the sciences, the social sciences, and the humanities. Published by the Institute for Scientific Information (Philadelphia), the *Science Citation Index* goes back to 1961 and currently covers more than 3,000 publications; the *Social Science Citation Index* begins with 1972 and indexes nearly 3,000 sources; the *Arts and Humanities Citation Index* starts with 1976 and currently covers more than 5,000 publications.

The indexes take their names from the "Citation Index" section, which enables a researcher to look up the name of an author to discover who has cited that author. The assumption is that others using the work of a particular researcher are doing related work. Using the "Permuterm Subject Index," the researcher can look for words which appear in titles of articles. In both cases, the entries are minimal and refer the user to a full entry in the "Source Index" portion, which includes a list of the references from each item cited. The "Source Index" functions as an author index for the time period covered. The citation indexes also include institutional indexes.

There are many advantages as well as some problems with this type of index. The multidisciplinary and extensive coverage of each citation index is useful for wide-ranging or interdisciplinary topics. The cited author approach enables the researcher to systematically access the literature through the reference structure, which has long been the preferred approach of many scholars. The keyword-in-title index is a convenient way to combine concepts and provides access through the same vocabulary used by authors. However, it also requires the researcher to search under every term authors might use in titles on a topic and titles that are not specific may be missed altogether. This problem is particularly frequent in the humanities, where titles are often clever or metaphoric rather than descriptive. In addition, the evaluative potential of citation counts has led to authors overzealously citing themselves or colleagues. Furthermore, those using citation indexes as an evaluative tool may fail to consider publications not covered by the indexes.

Identifying and Locating Periodical Articles

As noted in chapter 9, a strategy denotes both an overall plan for conducting library research on a subject and an approach for a particular type of information. A strategy for identifying periodical articles will include several steps: identifying relevant indexes, establishing vocabulary control, determining the coverage and best approach for each index, and maintaining careful records. At each step in the process, various tactics may be applied to counter difficulties.

When using a particular periodical index for the first time, the researcher should begin by consulting its introduction or user guide.

The procedure for studying reference books, outlined in chapter 2, is effective for becoming familiar with indexing publications. The index user should note the time period covered, the list of journals covered, and the arrangement. As most indexes use a variety of abbreviations, the user will also want to locate within the index lists of abbreviations, especially the abbreviations of periodical titles. Some indexes include special features, such as the listing of conference proceedings included in *Sociological Abstracts* or the annual review of key topics in *Environment Abstracts*. Other indexes provide unusual forms of access, such as the classification system used in the *Journal of Economic Literature* or the cited author and keyword-in-title indexes in citation indexes. When conventional indexes yield unsatisfactory results, one tactic is to seek more specialized types of access.

Periodical indexes provide access based on the materials covered, organization and types of access points, and subject headings. The coverage provided by an index can be very political, affecting both the market for a particular title and the researcher's perception of what is available. The way a source is organized and the forms of access (e.g., author, title, subject, keyword) affect not only the search itself, but also the user's conceptualization of the research problem. Subject headings may provide direct and comprehensive access to a topic, or they may be inconsistent and imprecise, scattering information and overlaying connotations.

Establishing vocabulary control for seeking periodical articles is even more complex than in the search for books, which is structured by a single controlled vocabulary and, with most online catalogs, words in book titles. Each periodical index, however, is based on a different controlled vocabulary, which may or may not be published. Headings may vary not only from index to index, but also from year to year within a particular index. The use of citation and computer-based indexes expands the possibilities to words in article titles as well, and, in most computer searches, words in abstracts may be searched.

The researcher's best tactic is both to brainstorm, generating a list of possible headings, and to consult any controlled vocabularies or thesauri that may be available for particular indexes or the subject area (see chapter 8). When no specific lists of subject headings are available, *The Library of Congress Subject Headings* can be consulted for suggestions. In addition, while using an index, the researcher should note any relevant *see* and *see also* references included in the index itself. Another tactic is to maintain a record of all search terms tried and those that were effective for each year of each index searched, in order to be thorough and consistent and to evaluate the access.

When using a print index, the student should begin with the issue or time period most relevant to the topic. Researchers often seek the most current information, but sometimes an earlier time period is more useful for a topic associated with a particular period. When the most recent information is not essential for a topic, a tactic may be to search a year or two retrospectively because the index will be cumulated and the periodicals are more likely to be on the shelves.

Careful record keeping is especially critical when using print indexes, as the search is likely to span indexes, terms, locations, and days. The value of bibliography, note, and vocabulary control cards (see chapter 7) becomes evident as citations are copied, serial listings are checked, journals are located, and articles are read and evaluated. A particularly useful tactic is to keep a record of the source of each citation so that incomplete or incorrect bibliography cards can be verified readily.

Many undergraduates assume that a periodical index is based on the particular library's collection. Because most indexes are produced commercially and used nationally, they will not reflect a particular library's serial holdings or locations. Researchers must determine how the particular library provides serial information. Serials may be listed in the card or online catalog. In an online catalog, periodical titles may be integrated with other materials, searchable as a format, or listed in a separate database. The serial listing may be a book, computer printout, microform, or some combination of formats. Periodicals may be shelved with the books or arranged separately. They may be in one location or dispersed among branch libraries. Current issues are likely to be shelved apart from bound volumes, which may be arranged by title or call number. When students are aware of the many possibilities, they know what questions to ask when using a library for the first time.

The Use and Evaluation of Periodical Articles

Students often resist the periodical literature because it is less familiar to them than books, appears difficult to locate, and usually cannot be checked out. However, students realize advantages of using articles once they learn how. For example, the shorter length of periodical articles means that students can read a larger number of authors and discover a wider variety of viewpoints.

However, as with books, periodical articles should be overviewed to confirm their relevance and appropriateness; they should also be critically evaluated. The overview process can usually be accomplished quickly and easily by reading an article's abstract, introduction, subheadings, and conclusion. While every author writes from a frame of reference that necessarily includes bias, some individuals make a conscious effort to minimize their personal biases, while others write to promote their point of view. The questions included in the four levels of critical evaluation (see chapter 10) provide a systematic approach for understanding and assessing an article, including its bias. The researcher may also want to examine the periodical to determine the perspective of the publication itself.

In addition to evaluating individual articles, researchers can consider the contribution of the periodical literature in general to the particular research project by asking the following questions:

> Is there a variety of indexes relevant to the subject?
> Do the indexes seem to cover all points of view?
> Is the topic easily accessed in the indexes?
> Are the subject headings descriptive?
> Do the headings collect or scatter relevant citations?
> Are there many citations for the topic?
> Does the library have a significant number of the periodicals cited?
> Of the titles available in the library, are the required issues on the shelves?
> What types of periodicals cover the subject?
> What kind of information is provided by each type?
> Are all points of view represented?
> What contribution do periodical articles make to the research project?

If the scholarly literature of a field is approached as conversations among experts, the research process may be seen as an opportunity to engage in discussion with experts. The researcher listens to the conversations by reading, and responds with a written product that conveys the essence of the researcher's own contribution to the discussion.

Sample Learning Objectives

Concepts to understand:

> The differences between popular, subject or professional, and scholarly periodicals.

The differences between general and subject indexes, and between standard, abstracting, and citation indexes.

The importance of consulting with a librarian to determine the best indexes for a topic.

The coverage provided by periodical indexes and the variety of access points.

The various options for determining periodical holdings in libraries.

The nature of periodical articles and their value in research.

The importance of overviewing and evaluating periodical articles.

Skills to apply:

Using periodical directories to identify periodicals published in a general subject area or in a geographic location.

Using print, microfilm, and CD-ROM periodical indexes to identify articles on a particular subject.

Locating periodical articles in the library.

Overviewing and evaluating articles.

Documenting and annotating articles.

Sample Class Discussion Questions

1. What are the characteristics and uses of popular magazines? Of professional or subject periodicals? Of scholarly journals?
2. How do you distinguish between a social scientist and a social commentator?
3. What is the value of footnotes and bibliographies in articles?
4. How can you decipher technical vocabulary?
5. What are some uses of periodical directories?
6. How can you determine the best indexes for a topic?
7. How can you identify nonmainstream or alternative materials on a subject?
8. How can you discover the coverage of a particular index?
9. What is a controlled vocabulary?
10. What is a citation? What is included in a typical citation?
11. What is an abstract?
12. How are abstracting indexes organized?
13. What types of access are provided in the citation indexes?
14. What are the advantages and disadvantages of the citation indexes?

15. How do you overview a periodical article?
16. How can you assess a periodical and an article within it?

Sample In-Class Activities

1. In small groups, students use periodical directories to identify periodicals on a subject and published in a given city. Each group reports to the class at large, commenting on the uses and value of periodical directories.
2. In small groups, students peruse copies of popular and scholarly periodicals. (Photocopies of popular and scholarly articles can be substituted; the articles might be on the same subject, although that is not necessary.) Each group responds to the following questions and reports back to the class at large.[5]

    Describe the general appearance and format of the periodicals.
    What is the purpose of each publication?
    Who are the intended audiences?
    Who are the contributors?
    Can you tell where the authors got their information?
    Can you detect any bias?
    How timely is the information?
    What can you tell about the financial structure of the publications?

3. Students work in small groups. Each group is given a copy of an index to examine by responding to the following questions. The groups report back to the class at large.

    What is the time period covered?
    What is the organization or arrangement?
    Does the index include any special features?
    What types of materials are indexed?
    What periodicals are indexed?
    Are there lists of abbreviations?
    What ways can you look up information?
    What can you tell about the subject headings used?
    What do the citations include?

4. Working in small groups, students critically evaluate a periodical article (see the four levels of critical evaluation in chapter 10).

Sample Take-Home Exercises

1. Students develop a strategy for identifying periodical articles on a topic. They determine what indexes to use and how best to take advantage of each index. They describe the process and assess the results, noting how they proceeded when results were unexpected or unsatisfactory. They also assess the library's coverage of their topic.
2. Students use a Wilson index, an abstracting index, and a nonprint index to look for articles on a particular topic. They compare the coverage, organization, and approach of the indexes.
3. Students assess an article by answering the questions in the four levels of critical evaluation and producing the results indicated.
4. Students identify articles on a topic by looking in periodical indexes. A sample procedure might include:

   a. Use a general index to identify popular periodical articles on a topic. Make bibliography cards for at least two to four articles. Locate and annotate at least two articles.
   b. Discuss the access to information on your topic in the popular press. Discuss the nature of the popular information on your topic. Describe how you critically evaluated these sources. What contribution did they make to your research?
   c. Identify the subject indexes available in the library relevant to your topic. Consult at least two indexes, at least one of which must be an abstracting index. List the title of each index you consulted, the time periods searched, the search terms you tried, and mark the subject headings that yielded the most citations.
   d. Make bibliography cards for at least three to six articles that sound useful. Each card should include a complete citation, the index in which the citation was listed, and a location and call number if the periodical is available on campus. Locate at least two to four of the articles. On the back of those cards, briefly summarize and evaluate the article. Engage thoughtfully in the annotation process, for this is a critical research

skill and a valuable learning technique as you distill the author's essence and personalize it for your own application.

e. Discuss the access to information on your topic in the scholarly literature. Discuss the nature of the scholarly information on your topic. Describe how you critically evaluated these sources. What contribution did they make to your research?

f. Compare the popular and scholarly sources.

Notes and Suggested Reading

1. Joan M. Bechtel, "Conversation, A New Paradigm for Librarianship?" *College and Research Libraries* 47:219 (May 1986).

2. Thelma Freides, *Literature and Bibliography of the Social Sciences* (Los Angeles: Melville, 1973), p. 2.

3. Ibid., pp. 3–4.

4. Bechtel, "Conversation, A New Paradigm for Librarianship?" p. 222.

5. Susan Anthes participated in the development of this and the next activities.

Chapter 13

Computerized
Information Access

It is well documented that advances in electronic technologies are transforming society, libraries, and research. Despite numerous and significant benefits, there are many problems associated with computerization. This chapter highlights a variety of issues related to computer use. The history of computerized information access in libraries is traced, and the online searching process is described.

Much of this discussion should be viewed as preliminary and provisional: preliminary because available resources and therefore appropriate coverage will vary from library to library, and provisional because anything recorded here, other than historical fact, will likely be out of date before its publication. Nevertheless, it is possible to suggest key areas to cover, leaving it up to teaching librarians to determine the most useful content for each situation and to update according to the current status of electronic advances. This chapter is therefore a starting point, to be augmented according to actual circumstances.

To whatever extent computer applications are covered in the classroom, the pedagogical principles of this course will hold. Active learning can be sustained by providing hands-on contact with computers in the library or other locations on campus, by having students complete computer-based search strategy worksheets, and even by simply letting students peruse directories of online databases to discover the quantity and variety of such sources.

Whether a search is actually executed or not, creative problem solving is applied when students generate terms for an online search and refine their search strategy. Critical evaluation can be called into play by having students assess the results of an online search (simulated or actual) and determine how to combine and integrate print and computerized sources.

Computers and Society

That illustrations of accelerating developments in electronic applications and computer miniaturization, power, and networking will no longer astound undergraduates testifies to the pervasiveness of electronic media and computers and belies their role in the advancement of a new age. Whether "new age" is used to denote music, human relations, spirituality, physics, biology, or the information society, little doubt remains that new approaches are gaining acceptance. According to Priscella Norton, electronic technologies are a part of this shift:

> The media present us with a paradigm of how to think that is nondiscursive, presentational, subjective, emotive, and nonrational. . . . [The] structure of a computer environment creates habits of thought that may be characterized as tentative, flexible, connected, patterned, relational, and predictive.[1]

It is easy to extoll the advantages and marvels of the computer but important to address the dark side as well. Throughout this book, computer-based options for identifying sources and preparing information are covered. The benefits and dangers of computerization in libraries and research parallel the benefits and dangers of computers in society generally.

Many business functions, including record-keeping, communications, and decision-making processes, have been automated to maximize profits and minimize costs. In industry, computers are used to process materials, control production, and maintain specifications with great consistency. Workers in these areas, however, may experience feelings of depersonalization, alienation, and fear of unemployment.[2]

On all educational levels, computer-assisted instruction (CAI) is used for drill-and-practice, tutorials, and simulation. Software is shared and marketed nationally, but this approach is frequently challenged pedagogically. Most applications are no more than a new context for traditional methods of teaching rather than a fresh and invigorating approach to learning. Critics also fear that students are being trained to rely on computers rather than to develop their own skills.

Research in artificial intelligence (AI) is one of the most controversial applications of computers. AI is the use of computers for problem-solving functions as well as the study of human thought processes; robotics is an evolving area of AI. Computers have been programmed to play games, prove mathematical theorems, and study language, but opponents maintain that human intelligence cannot and should not be simulated by machines.³

In department stores, automated cash registers perform sales transactions and inventory control. In supermarkets, manufacturers' bar code labels enable checkout computers to look up and tabulate prices. (Similar labels are used to check out library books.) At automated tellers, electronic fund transfer systems offer a variety of services. In hospitals, both record keeping and medical evaluation are electronically facilitated.

To what extent are the efficiency and convenience afforded by computers offset by the potential for privacy violations and computer crime? As medical, financial, government, and marketing databases increase in size and detail, individual concerns for privacy also increase. Because the government has computerized records of the Census Bureau, the Federal Bureau of Investigation, and the National Security Agency, among others, many foresee the rise of "Big Brother."

Despite security measures, false information may be generated with computers, data may be deleted or altered, telecommunication systems can be invaded, and hardware and software can be sabotaged. Even intentionally innocent pranks, such as inserting a time-delayed message into a software program, can have serious consequences, as the epidemic of computer "viruses" demonstrates. While individuals are more likely to be alarmed about crimes committed with computers, software manufacturers grow increasingly concerned about copyright violations as users freely duplicate programs.

Extensive computer use has also raised health concerns. The video-display terminals (VDTs) that most computer operators use shoot an electronic beam at the video screen with high-voltage currents. They generate weak X-rays, ultraviolet and other types of radiation, infrared light, and other electromagnetic fields. Static electricity and ultra-high-pitched sounds have been attributed to VDTs. Irritability, stress, rashes, headaches, dizziness, eyestrain, blurred vision, cataracts, miscarriages, and birth defects have all been blamed on VDT exposure.⁴ While studies on computer-based health hazards are inconclusive, ergonomic adjustments often reduce the effects. Heavy computer use is also suspected for disrupting biorhythms, time perception, and psychological health.

The machinery of politics has been altered by computing machinery. Political parties on a state level analyze and plot districts, pinpoint special interest groups, and conduct direct mailings based on preprogrammed data analysis. Computer-tabulated polls are used both to determine and to influence public opinion. As the government increasingly relies on computers for weapons control and crisis management, the risks become staggering. In short, as Roszak proclaims:

> This promising technology—itself a manifestation of prodigious human imagination and inventiveness—is being degraded into a means of surveillance and control, of financial and managerial centralization, of manipulating public opinion, of making war. The presence of personal computers in millions of homes, especially when they are used as little more than trivial amusements, does not in any meaningful way offset the power the machine brings to those who use it for these purposes.[5]

Computers and Research

The proliferation of scholars and the application of computers to research have created both information overload and intensified pressure to publish and be positioned on the cutting edge of research.[6] Libraries, as well as individuals, recognize the impossibility of acquiring all the information on any area of study. For the individual it is simply too much to identify and absorb; for libraries it is too much to afford, given rising costs and diminishing budgets, as well as too much to store, given limited building space.

Electronic technologies are reshaping both the approach to and the dissemination of research. Computer applications to the research process appear limitless. Supercomputers, capable of more than 100 million operations per second, are used in aerodynamics, seismology, meteorology, and nuclear and plasma physics for numerical simulations of physical systems. In scientific laboratories, computer interfaces program and monitor instruments and collect and analyze data. Computerized radiotelemetry devices are implanted in research animals to monitor location, temperature, blood flow, strain, and so on. Medical researchers study computer simulations of disease processes, physiologic mechanisms, and pharmacological interactions. Rapid and multiple computer manipulations of geographic data add new dimensions to cartography. Scholars in the social sciences and humanities apply computerized language analysis to study political documents, presidential rhetoric, the psychological patterns of suicide notes, Shakespeare, and the Bible. Computerized information access eases the work of bibliographic research and makes it possible to identify sources of information from one's desk.

Equally remarkable are advances and possibilities in the communication and dissemination of research. Researchers take advantage of computer software not only to process words and manipulate data, but also to generate and organize ideas, outline, edit, and proofread. Manuscripts are transmitted to publishers and revised on disks or through telecommunications and, increasingly, researchers communicate among themselves with electronic networks and bulletin boards.

As illustrated in chapter 1, this development can eliminate stages in the cycle of information processing. Electronic shortcuts offer benefits to the researcher, but also pose potential short circuits to the flow of information. Information may become exclusively available to members of an elite computer network, and hard copy may escape formal publication. Also problematical is the loss of provisional documentation, as early versions and ongoing revisions cease to exist electronically. The library's role in the collection and preservation of such records may be abrogated. Thus, the new technologies pose new problems as well as exciting possibilities.

Among the exciting possibilities is the emerging, and already partially realized, scholar's workstation, or integrated array of electronic resources supporting all steps of the research process from a desk top. With a microcomputer linked locally and internationally, the researcher's software library could facilitate conceptualization, information searching and retrieval, communication with other researchers, data manipulation, organization, writing, editing, formatting, transmittal for publication, and feedback. While the workstation concept promises greater efficiency in research, it does not eliminate the need for research skill development, because the intellectual dynamics of the research process remain the same despite the accoutrements.

Computers and Libraries

Computers have been used in libraries since the early 1960s. Applications range from standard microcomputer functions to acquisitions, cataloging, and circulation tasks, and include computer networks, on-line catalogs, and computerized information access; telefacsimile technology for document delivery is an emerging area.[7] Many online catalogs are still in developmental or transitional stages and must be used in combination with the existing card catalog. Computerized information access means searching with a computer the machine-readable versions of printed indexing and abstracting publications, databases without printed equivalents, and a growing number of specialized online sources, including newspapers, encyclopedias, and directories. Such access may be online or on compact disc.

A History of Computerized Information Access

Online database searching was parented by the information explosion and computer technologies. Although some tentative batch searching of bibliographic records was performed in the 1950s, the first on-demand search service was offered by the National Library of Medicine in the early 1960s with MEDLARS (Medical Literature Analysis and Retrieval System). According to Bourne:

> The average NLM in-house turnaround time was about two weeks, and the access time for the user was about six weeks. If the search formulation was incorrect, or the results unsatisfactory, then the cycle had to be repeated.[8]

Other demonstrations of limited batch searching systems were featured in the early 1960s, including System Development Corporation's (SDC) program and Lockheed's service to NASA using the DIALOG system. By 1965, Chemical Abstracts Service issued *Chemical and Biological Activities* in both print and magnetic tape, which stimulated the provision of magnetic tape by other index publishers as well as the Library of Congress.[9]

Lockheed provided full service to NASA by 1967; by 1969 it began to offer online access to the Office of Education's ERIC file. The fledgling NASA file included 260,000 citations and ERIC included some 20,000.[10] Neufeld and Cornog note:

> Throughout the 1960s, the U.S. government had led the conversion of bibliographic files to machine-readable formats, followed closely by some of the scientific societies that publish A&I [abstracting and indexing] services (American Petroleum Institute, American Society for Metals, CAS) and a few for-profit companies (Institute for Scientific Information, Derwent)....During the first half of the 1970s, nearly all the major A&I services began to computerize their operations with a view to cutting production costs and time lags for print products as much as to provide online access.[11]

In the early 1970s, online services expanded commercially with increased files and vendors. DIALOG added nongovernmental databases, and SDC and Bibliographic Retrieval Services (BRS) became market forces. A DIALOG spin-off became the Information Retrieval

Service (IRS), Europe's largest search service. New entries into the indexing field, such as Congressional Information Service and Predicasts, used computer publishing technologies for print sources and made the computer tape byproducts available through DIALOG, SDC, or BRS.[12]

By the middle 1970s, the online information industry, now including text and numeric as well as bibliographic databases, was duly recognized by professional associations, publications, and conferences. Database coverage spread to the social sciences, and special and academic libraries became users. Neufeld and Cornog note that a "new profession was born: the online searcher, or 'intermediary.'"

"Diversification," according to the same authors, "was the most important trend for databases during 1975–1980."[13] Files became available for the humanities, business, and the popular audience. Numeric and full-text files increased, and directory and other nonbibliographic referral databases appeared. More libraries offered online searching, and both online vendors and database producers provided online training.

In an early ARL handbook on online search services, David Wax noted:

> Computer-based bibliographic search services were not widely available in academic libraries prior to 1973. . . . However, since 1973 on-line search services in a wide range of disciplines have been introduced into many academic libraries and this trend is likely to continue. This growth is illustrated by an informal poll taken at the May, 1976 meeting of the Association of Research Libraries which indicated that approximately 80 percent of ARL libraries currently offer on-line searching via one or both of the major commercial vendors.[14]

Widespread use of computer databases brought general concern about issues related to this search mode. A fee versus free debate ensued, underlining libraries' traditional commitment to equal information access. The commercialization of information also has far-reaching implications for libraries as well as society. John Haar maintains that:

> Whatever the current inequities, they pale before the potential for abuses in this area. The greatest danger lies in the realization that the control of databases carries with it the power to manipulate them.[15]

Such issues remain unresolved through the 1980s, and it is clear their significance will deepen, for the computer searching industry and library search services continue to grow and expand to an overwhelming extent. Continuing technological advances in telecommunications, terminals, modems, and printers contribute to the increased use. The Cuadra/Elsevier *Directory of Online Databases* has provided an ongoing record of industry growth since 1979–1980. At that time there were 400 databases offered by 221 producers through 59 services. Those numbers had more than quadrupled by 1983–1984, with 1,878 databases, 927 producers, and 272 services. The quantities nearly doubled in 1988 with 3,699 databases, 1,685 producers, and 555 services.[16]

However, the directory publishers noted that the number of new databases added in 1987 was more than 20 percent fewer than the number of files that were added in 1986. The 27 new online services in 1987 represent 36 percent of the growth in 1986 and 29 percent during 1985. The slowdown may be attributable to the growth of gateways, which increased from 35 in 1986 to 59 in 1987.[17]

The *Directory of Online Databases* defines a gateway as:

> Any computer service that acts as an intermediary between a user and the databases resident on the computers of one or more other organizations. There are several classes of gateways. Some gateways are also online services, i.e., they also have databases resident on their own computers. Others, which do not have resident databases, may simply pass users through to the online service of the users choice or they may provide a "front-end" (software) interface to help users to select and use the appropriate databases and services. In addition, some gateways are essentially "transparent" to users, who may not know when they have been switched to another computer. In some cases, some of the databases offered through a particular online service may *not* be available to users who access the computer through a gateway service.[18]

The gateway marks a major transition in the online industry to the home computer market or end user. The end user performs searches directly rather than through a trained intermediary. End users, including students, professionals, and the general public, may themselves subscribe to an online service or access a service provided by a library. Even secondary and elementary students are learning online searching through new services offered to schools by database vendors.

Another advance in computerized searching is the compact disc–read only memory, or CD-ROM. CD-ROM is one of several optical disc formats. Optical technology is used to record audio, video, and data text on computer disks with lasers. The 8″ or 12″ video discs are used to store sound and images and promise exciting educational applications. The compact disc, introduced in 1983, is 4³/₄″ and stores digital data (audio CDs achieved rapid popularity for home listening). CD-ROMs are loaded into a disk drive and accessed with a microcomputer. They hold some 550 million characters, or the equivalent of 1,500 low-density floppy disks or 275,000 double-spaced typed pages. The twenty-one volumes of the Grolier encyclopedia, for example, take up less than a fifth of a compact disc.

Traditional print publishers and specialized library publishers (e.g., Wilson and Bowker) are promoting CD-ROM publications as are optical publishers, such as Silver Platter, who acquire databases, such as ERIC. This computerized format is popular in libraries, despite the high cost and the fact that the discs do not cumulate. They do offer students the opportunity to access information using the same search principles and computer-based technology of online databases.

Online Services

The major online systems remain DIALOG, ORBIT (SDC), and BRS. The vendors that make them available buy databases from various producers and sell subscription access to libraries, other organizations, and individuals. DIALOG included 280 files as of 1988, ORBIT some 100 databases, and BRS more than 145.

There are two types of databases: reference and text. Reference databases, equivalent to "finding" reference sources, are used to identify sources of information. Bibliographic reference databases provide citations and, in some cases, abstracts of materials, including periodical articles, books, dissertations, and government publications. Examples of bibliographic databases include the *Social Science Citation Index* and *Psychological Abstracts*. Referral databases are another type of reference database. They provide listings of organizations, individuals, products, services, etc.; examples are the *Electronic Yellow Pages* and *International Software Database*.

Text or source databases, equivalent to "fact" reference works, contain the full text of information sources, such as periodicals, newspapers, news wire services, encyclopedias, and census and other demographic reports. They may provide text, numeric data, or a combination of the two. Examples include the *Harvard Business Review*, the *Academic American Encyclopedia*, and *Disclosure*.

The full range of online files and searching options are available in the services provided to trained professionals; end-user services include a subset of the files and a simplified and less sophisticated command structure that is sometimes menu-based. Both types of services include printed documentation and database descriptions. An increasing number of libraries are training end users and offering that level of service for less cost than searches that require reference staff.

There are many reasons why computerized access to information has become the preferred approach and will continue to grow. Compared to manual searching, online access usually saves the user a considerable amount of searching time: it is often said that what takes an hour to search manually will take only one minute online. Computer-based searching also offers a greater variety of access points. While print indexes typically provide access by subject headings and authors only, database access includes words in titles and abstracts as well as in virtually any field (or unit of information) within the records. In addition, terms can be combined or limited, by year or language, for example, with greater facility online. Databases are more current than print indexes, and some online sources list materials that are not included in their print counterparts. A growing number of databases is available only online with no print equivalent.

In some subject areas, however, particularly within the humanities, there are few or no databases available. Often online indexes do not go as far back in time as the print version. A search for a limited number of materials on a precise and well-indexed topic may not warrant a computer search. The most restrictive disadvantage to online searching is the fact that it is usually a fee-based service. Telecommunications charges remain prohibitive enough to most libraries that they must charge users for all or some of the costs incurred. The necessity and appropriateness of this practice continue to be widely discussed among librarians, but most users can expect to pay for this service. The advent of reduced price end-user services offers one solution for libraries to reduce their rates or subsidize the service.

A basic vocabulary is required to understand computer literature searching. A dictionary of more than one hundred pages, including titles of individual databases, is provided in *Online Searching: A Dictionary and Bibliographic Guide*.[19] Briefer but clear and concise glossaries of online terms are offered by Dialog Information Services in their guides to searching DIALOG and Knowledge Index. Current, comprehensive information on the search process is provided in the published documentation made available by the search services.

Conducting a Computerized Search

To conduct a computerized search, whether through an intermediary or end-user service or with a CD-ROM, the searcher begins by developing a search strategy. Most libraries provide a search strategy worksheet to structure this process. The topic should be stated as clearly and precisely as possible. Focused topics are generally more successful. The topic statement is then analyzed to specify the concepts. Two to four concepts are optimum: a single concept indicates a too general topic, and more than three or four concepts would make a search unwieldy.

The next step is to generate a list of synonyms for each concept. The researcher can brainstorm to enumerate known words, but should also consult thesauri to extend the list and to determine actual descriptors. Some database descriptors are based on standard controlled vocabularies, such as *The Library of Congress Subject Headings*, and others are drawn from a thesaurus created for the database. In the latter case, the controlled vocabulary may be available as a print or online publication. An alternative to consulting thesauri is to begin with a free-text search and then to peruse online records to select descriptors from those assigned to relevant documents.

Truncation allows the searcher to input the root of a word in order to retrieve all terms beginning with those letters. For example, typing the letters "librar" would retrieve the words library, libraries, librarian, and librarianship. This feature must be used with care, however, for it is easy to overlook irrelevant words that may begin with the same letters as relevant terms.

Relationships among concepts and among terms are indicated with logical operators or Boolean logic. The vertical strings of equivalent terms are connected with the OR operator, while the horizontal lists, each representing a concept, are connected with the AND operator. In some systems, the connectors are imbedded in the search structure or menu-prompted.

Online systems are dialed up with a manual or automated protocol to access a service through a telecommunications network. A CD-ROM may already be loaded or need to be inserted into a CD drive; the source is then activated with one or several keystrokes of a microcomputer. The search is conducted with a command language, which may be quite extensive and highly sophisticated, such as DIALOG or ORBIT, or readily apparent and menu-driven, as seen in most end-user services and CD-ROMs. The beauty of computerized searches is their interactiveness—they can be continuously revised based on the results.

Results are displayed on the screen. They may be printed out as the search proceeds; selected items may be printed at the conclusion of the search; or the results may be downloaded and printed after logging off the system. The printout is interpreted much like any index entry, but the format may appear unfamiliar to the student.

Integration and Evaluation of Computerized Sources

The challenge when instructing researchers in computerized access is not in convincing them of the value of these sources—most students are ready converts—or in teaching the techniques, but rather in teaching the appropriate integration and evaluation of databases. Researchers should not turn to the computer because it provides the easiest or fastest access, but because it is the most appropriate and effective source for an information need. Students also must be alerted to the problematical aspects of computerized information access.[20]

When research is approached with a search strategy, the full array of sources, both print and computerized, is considered. Access sources are selected to provide well-rounded coverage of the topic. All sources, regardless of format, are critically evaluated. With databases, the print documentation is reviewed to determine the scope, coverage, periodicals included, vocabulary control, and so on, as well as the particulars of the searching capabilities. This process is essentially no different from that applied to the critical evaluation of print periodical indexes.

Students may be more or less likely to review the hard-copy output of a computerized search in terms of search effectiveness because it exists as a formal product rather than their own scribblings. The inclusion of irrelevant material in a printout or an absence of known items may point to the absolute literalism of the computer or the vagaries of indexing. Because computer searching is dazzling in its mechanization of a cumbersome process, but prone to the problems and politics of any access source, it is essential to critically evaluate the results.

Sample Learning Objectives

Concepts to understand:

The variety and pervasiveness of computer applications.
The problems and dangers of computer use.

The scholar's workstation.
Computer applications in libraries.
The development of computerized information access.
Database vendors.
Reference versus text databases.
Intermediary-based versus end-user searching.
CD-ROM sources.
The online search process.

Skills to apply:

Developing an online search strategy.
Conducting an online or CD-ROM search.
Analyzing the results of an online or CD-ROM printout.

Sample Class Discussion Questions

1. What are some changes brought about by increased computer use?
2. What are some of the dangers of increased computer use?
3. Do you agree with John Naisbett, author of *Megatrends*, that "high touch" will offset the depersonalization of "high tech"?
4. To what extent and on what levels should computer-based methods of teaching and learning be incorporated in the schools?
5. Is the human brain comparable to a computer? What are the moral and ethical implications of this analogy?
6. How do you think individual privacy can be protected as more and more information about individuals is stored on computers?
7. What should be the sanctions against computer crime?
8. Should the United States continue to automate weapons and crisis management?
9. Do you think, as Theodore Roszak claims, that our society has become a "cult" of information?
10. Should researchers be required to submit hard copy of their research in process to preserve the developmental record?
11. Should researchers' electronic networks be regulated to ensure equal access?
12. What computer applications are you aware of in this library?
13. Should libraries charge a fee for online database searching?
14. How can you effectively integrate the print and computerized sources available for a particular topic?

Sample In-Class Activities

1. The class visits a campus computer lab for an introduction to the personal computer or word processing.
2. The class observes a demonstration of a library computer application, such as circulation or OCLC.
3. In small groups, students peruse a directory of online databases, looking for databases relevant to a particular topic but also noting the wide range and variety of available databases.
4. Students complete or assess a search strategy worksheet for a particular topic.
5. Working in pairs, one student assumes the role of intermediary and the other of researcher. The intermediary interviews the researcher about a particular information need and develops a search strategy for the topic, which is assessed by the researcher. Students then switch roles.
6. In small groups, students analyze a simulated search strategy worksheet and the resultant printout.
7. The whole class works in groups of two pairs. Two pairs of students seek information on the same topic; one pair uses a computerized source and the other a print index. Both pairs compare their results and the process they used, and then report back to the class at large.

Sample Take-Home Exercises

1. Students submit evidence of learning a computer application, such as word processing or spreadsheet.
2. Students complete a search strategy worksheet and execute an online or CD-ROM search. They assess the process and results by (1) evaluating the print documentation for the database; (2) evaluating the search strategy based on the relevance of items retrieved and a comparison of the search terms to the descriptors assigned to useful items; and (3) determining whether expected items were retrieved.
3. Students compare a search on a particular topic in a print and computer-based source (same or different indexes).
4. Students interpret the citations and locate some of the items listed in a computer search printout.

Notes and Suggested Reading

1. Priscella Norton, "An Agenda for Technology and Education: Eight Imperatives," *Educational Technology* 25:17 (Jan. 1985).

2. Nancy Stern and Robert A. Stern, *Computers in Society* (Englewood Cliffs, N.J.: Prentice-Hall, 1983), pp. 237–274.

3. Ibid., pp. 275–304, 331–348.

4. Art Kleiner, "The Health Hazards of Computers: A Guide to Worrying Intelligently," *Whole Earth Review* 48:82 (Fall 1985).

5. Theodore Roszak, *The Cult of Information: The Folklore of Computers and the True Art of Thinking* (New York: Pantheon, 1986), p. 218.

6. ARL Task Force on Scholarly Information, "The Changing System of Scholarly Communication" (Washington, D.C.: Association of Research Libraries, Mar. 1986).

7. For a discussion of the impact of these developments, see Barbara B. Moran, *Academic Libraries: The Changing Knowledge Centers of Colleges and Universities*, ASHE-ERIC Higher Education Research Report No. 8 (Washington, D.C.: Association for the Study of Higher Education, 1984), pp. 6–28.

8. Charles P. Bourne, "On-line Systems: History, Technology, and Economics," *Journal of the American Society for Information Science* 31:155 (May 1980).

9. M. Lynne Neufeld and Martha Cornog, "Database History: From Dinosaurs to Compact Discs," *Journal of the American Society for Information Science* 37:183 (July 1986).

10. Bourne, "On-line Systems," p. 156.

11. Neufeld and Cornog, "Database History," p. 184.

12. Ibid.

13. Ibid., p. 186.

14. David M. Wax, *A Handbook for the Introduction of On-line Bibliographic Search Services into Academic Libraries*, Office of University Library Management Studies Occasional Papers Number 4 (Washington, D.C.: Association of Research Libraries, 1976).

15. John M. Haar, "The Politics of Information: Libraries and Online Retrieval Systems," *Library Journal* 111:42 (1 Feb. 1986).

16. "Preface," *Directory of Online Databases* 9:v (Jan. 1988).

17. "Directory Shows Slowdown in Growth of Online Databases," *Information Today: The Newspaper for Users and Producers of Electronic Information Services* 5:1 (Apr. 1988).

18. "Introduction," *Directory of Online Databases* 9:viii (Jan. 1988).

19. Greg Byerly, *Online Searching: A Dictionary and Bibliographic Guide* (Littleton, Colo.: Libraries Unlimited, 1983).

20. Harold B. Shill, "Bibliographic Instruction: Planning for the Electronic Information Environment," *College and Research Libraries* 48:446 (Sept. 1987).

Chapter *14*

Government Publications

Susan Anthes

Almost one-fifth of American workers are employed by one form of government or another. Many of their jobs involve collecting and producing information, much of which is used to determine policies and laws. Government information is crucial for assessing the multifaceted problems of contemporary society, but it is often overlooked by researchers. While different from other library materials, government publications are often highly useful in research. Where possible, library classes should have the opportunity to meet with a government documents librarian or visit a government documents collection.

Government publications are defined here as those items published by any governmental agency, whether local, regional, national, or international. They may be pamphlets, serials, books, or nonprint materials. The U.S. government disseminates its publications through depository libraries and publishes *The Monthly Catalog*, the primary index to those publications. Commercial publishers, notably the Congressional Information Service, also provide access to government publications. Researchers must use a variety of guides and indexes to identify the full range of materials produced by governments and international organizations.

Students will find the variety, timeliness, and authority of government publications useful for most research topics, but government publications are as prone to bias as any others and must be carefully evaluated for effective application. Students should also be aware of the larger social and legal factors that influence the production and availability of government publications.

Susan Anthes is currently Assistant Science Librarian and Map Curator at the University of Colorado, Boulder, Libraries.

Dissemination and Indexing

Government publications have been in existence as long as there have been governments. Until the end of the nineteenth century, there was little attempt in the United States to disseminate or index systematically any government-produced information except legislative reports. In 1895, the Federal Depository Library Act established a distribution system for federal publications. The law states that libraries declared "depository libraries" may receive single copies of all U.S. government publications not designated as "classified." A major responsibility of the depository library is then to provide free and open access to these publications for any library user. The intent of the legislation is to provide for better government through an informed citizenry.

Each state is allowed to have two "regional depository" libraries. These are required to accept one copy of all documents and may not withdraw or throw away older documents without permission of the Superintendent of Documents. Partial depositories may select only the documents thought to be appropriate for their collection. These partial depository libraries may have only 5 to 10 percent of available publications. While depository status can be a tremendous source of "free" material, it does cost the participating library staff time, shelf space, and other overhead costs. There are now over one hundred regional depository libraries around the country and hundreds of partial depositories, even some in foreign countries.

At the same time the federal government started the depository system, it recognized the need to index the publications produced. The *Monthly Catalog of U.S. Government Publications* has been published since 1895, and it continues to provide basic access to government information. The catalog has grown in size and changed in format over the years, but it remains the essential index for searching government information.

The *Monthly Catalog* began as a small index with only minimal keyword access; there was no author or title index. Because many government publications, such as legislative materials, do not have a standard or formal title and are often authored by an agency or department rather than an individual, the lack of such indexes was not thought to be a problem. However, without some sort of structured indexing system, the documents were often erratically indexed, and access was difficult. In 1976, when the *Monthly Catalog* began to be produced by computer, each item was entered as it was fully cataloged by the Library of Congress. Each document, even if it was only a two-page pamphlet, now had at least an author, title, and several subject heading entries. This change was an important step forward in the accessibility of government information.

Types of Government Documents

The smallest of local governments produces documents that may cover local statistics, laws and regulations, and issues of regional importance. These documents are probably most often collected by local public libraries; they also can be obtained from the specific government or agency. Regional networks or associations of governments that work together on issues such as transportation, conservation, and economic development often publish useful information which can also be located through the agency offices or local documents collections.

States also publish documents, and many states have set up their own depository system based on the federal system. Some states have depositories outside their own borders. State publications can be useful in studying problems unique to one state, comparing statistics or programs, or looking at an individual state's innovative method of handling a governmental problem. Most state, regional, and local documents have very little in the way of indexing tools; the best source is often the person or librarian who works directly with them.

As indicated above, the largest collections of documents in U.S. libraries are federal publications. Published by the Superintendent of Documents and distributed through the depository system, most of these publications come from specific agencies of the federal government, such as the Bureau of Land Management or the Department of the Interior. They address issues of concern to the agencies and cover almost every subject imaginable. Federal documents are very accessible through the indexing and abstracting tools now available.

The legal records of the federal legislature, the courts, and the regulatory agencies represent a special type of government information. All laws passed by the U.S. Congress are recorded in a chronological listing in the *United States Statutes at Large*; laws are also codified by subject in the *United States Code*. In addition, the *United States Reports* provides a complete chronological listing of all decisions of the United States Supreme Court. Lower federal and state courts have comparable sets of records for their proceedings. Regulatory agencies, or those enabled by legislation to make rules to carry out specific legislation, have their rules and regulations listed chronologically in the *Federal Register* and codified by subject in the *Code of Federal Regulations*. Legal information is an important subset of government information, and more can be learned about it in various guides to the literature.

The federal government also funds many research projects at universities and research institutes around the country. When a research project receives federal funding, the researchers are required to write a report describing the results; these "technical reports" form a large body of invaluable social and scientific research information. Although this information is not part of the depository system, many libraries have collections of such material.

Foreign governments and international organizations also publish official material according to their own unique publishing and distributing schemes. Some foreign governments, such as Great Britain and Canada, have their own publishing, distributing, and indexing systems. In order to use materials from these governments, it is necessary to understand the publishing system of each one. The same is true for international organizations, such as the United Nations and the European Economic Community.

Government information comes in all types of physical formats. Federal government material may be simple pamphlets, such as the ones that describe each national park, or in-depth studies on national health care issues. The government publishes journals and magazines, such as the *Monthly Labor Review*, as well as information issued once every ten years, such as the *Decennial Census*. Government information appears in microformat and even on compact disc; the federal government has published photographs, maps, comic books, films, and recordings. Because of the wide variety of formats, it is difficult to file government documents in standard library stacks. Thus, many libraries house their documents collection in a separate location.

The Value of Government Publications

The United States government is the single largest publisher in the world. Comprehensive collections of government publications can contain several million items. The government publishes information on all aspects of our lives; it collects more statistics about our life and country than any other organization. One decennial census requires thousands of pages to report the collected statistics, including such items as the number of televisions per household, number of miles traveled to work, and the number of bathtubs per block in cities.

Federal information is not protected by copyright and thus can be quoted and used freely. It can be either primary source material coming directly from government agencies, or it can be secondary source material compiled and republished from outside sources. Government publications, of course, contain the primary record of the workings of Congress and provide the legislative history and intent as well as the wording of the laws themselves. Voting records, speeches, and other relevant material can be found in the *Congressional Record*. Congressional hearings contain verbatim testimony from expert witnesses called by Congress to answer important questions pertinent to the issues being studied. Such direct questions and answers from significant participants are often difficult to find elsewhere.

Since the government conducts and sponsors much scientific research, government documents are a vast repository of scientific information. Not only does the government publish the technical reports from this research, it also publishes a full record of each patent granted in the United States. Agencies such as the Environmental Protection Agency publish environmental impact statements that are detailed reviews of federally funded projects and developments affecting the environment.

Access to government information may be vital for the student, researcher, businessperson, and citizen. The government publishes tremendous amounts of statistical material useful to the business world for analysis, as well as information for the citizen interested in doing business with the government. The government is often in the forefront of research on important issues, and frequently releases reports before they appear in commercial publications. Full participation in a democracy is dependent upon knowledge of government activities.

Accessing Government Publications

Since libraries typically keep government publications in a separate collection, these publications are not usually entered in the card catalog or serial catalog of the library and therefore are not easily accessible to students. The publications, particularly federal documents, have their own classification and numbering system. The Superintendent of Documents Classification System, based on department and agency divisions of government, is used most often. Students need to be aware of this different system and recognize that it is simply another means of accessing particular publications. Some libraries with large documents collections have other classification or numbering systems for documents from state, foreign, and international agencies. Schmeckebier's *Government Publications and Their Use* is the standard reference book for understanding government publications collections.[1]

In order to access government publications, students need a basic understanding of government organization. Since most government information is classified and arranged by department and agency, identification of appropriate agencies is important. For the federal government, the *United States Manual* describes all sections and agencies under each department and provides names, addresses, and telephone numbers. This publication comes out every year and is the best place to begin research. Since most states publish organization manuals, students should be encouraged to look at these sources as well. If a library does not have a collection of government documents, the *U.S. Manual* and state organization manuals can be used to write directly for publications.

As mentioned above, the most important index and access tool for federal information is the *Monthly Catalog of United States Government Publications*. This monthly index is cumulated annually, has had further cumulations for some years, and goes back to 1895. As noted, it has gone through several format changes. Library of Congress subject headings are used as well as some free-text terms. A title and author index has also been available since 1976. Before then, there was very little standardization in the subject access to government documents.

Some libraries include their collection of government documents in an online catalog, making documents much more accessible to library users. Searching by computer usually provides better free-text access, especially for current topics. Although their availability will vary from library to library, there are many additional access sources for government information.

Recently, private publishers have begun to produce tools providing access to government information. Products similar to the printed *Monthly Catalog* are now available in microfilm, both from the government and from private publishers. For example, the *Congressional Information Service* indexes and abstracts all publications of the United States Congress. It describes individual testimony in congressional hearings, lists material submitted as evidence, and provides an excellent source for research on legislation. The *American Statistics Index* provides access to the millions of government statistics collected and published each year. This tool also contains abstracts detailing the type of charts and statistics available in each publication.

Access to nonfederal collections is much more erratic. CIS currently publishes an index entitled *Index to International Statistics*, but there is little else for access to international collections. Many organizations publish their own catalog or index to their publications. Some states also have some type of index or checklist for their publications, but this varies with the state and library.

Social and Legal Implications

The Federal Depository Act indicates the government's concern for providing information for an informed citizenry. However, directives from the Reagan administration reduced the number and availability of federal documents in the depository program. The purported aim of such reductions is to make federal publishing more cost effective and efficient; however, the overall effect has been to limit the availability of government information. The federal government has encouraged the private sector to publish and distribute more and more government information. This trend has resulted in higher prices for services and publications formerly supplied by the federal government. In essence, the information has become a commodity, sometimes a high-priced one. An increasing number of documents is coming out only in microformat, which has been strongly resisted by the general public. Computerized information is better received, but it is less readily provided by most libraries.[2] More and more of the government's information is classified, thus unavailable to the public for long periods of time. Questions concerning what should be classified and when, and who should have access to classified material and when, are being raised by these new policies.

Government information is collected, produced, and distributed using tax dollars from the citizens of the United States. This fact alone has major implications for the availability and accessibility of information. Citizens have a right to know how their money is spent, what their legislators are doing, and what business opportunities there are with the federal government. When a library in a private college is named a depository, that library must keep its documents collection open to the public, even if the rest of the library is not. Because the documents are theoretically only on deposit from the government, it is a federal crime to steal or mutilate these publications. There also have been instances of federal agents attempting to remove certain documents from collections because of their sensitive nature.

Some government information is currently being lost in the electronic publishing process. Legislative history is no longer as accurate and detailed because versions of bills and amendments are no longer printed every time changes are made. When the change is entered into the electronic record, the old version is never seen again. The course of legislation is hard to trace and thus so is the legislative intent of the sponsors and adversaries of the bill.

There is controversy around the free and open access libraries provide to government information. Charges have been made that foreign governments can access all they need to know to compete with the United States. Charges have also been raised that dangerous weapons, even nuclear weapons, can be designed and built (except for the fuel) using technical report collections in government documents libraries. By the same token, average citizens can use federally funded research to produce their own inventions, which may be worth a lot of money. Should libraries or the federal government restrict access to information that citizens pay for? Is there a national security concern?

Students should also be aware that government information may be biased. Agencies may not want to publish information or statistics that do not reflect well on their performance. It was only through diligent use of the Freedom of Information laws that so-called whistle-blowers were able to prove charges of incredible waste by some of the government's defense contractors. The *Congressional Record* is supposed to provide an accurate word-by-word account of activities on the floor of the Senate and the House of Representatives. In fact, any senator or representative has three days to make changes in the day's report. They can speak one way on the floor and have the record show the opposite way if they wish. They also have the privilege of submitting anything they want to the record, even their favorite apple pie recipes.

The Freedom of Information Act, passed in 1966 and strengthened in 1974, allows private citizens access to much government information that is never published. Records of meetings, contracts, minutes, memoranda, even FBI surveillance reports and hearings, may be available only in agency files. These records can be requested. Each request is considered on an individual basis, but requests have been denied, sometimes for seemingly capricious reasons. The most commonly cited reason for denial of access is national security. This denial raises the issue of conflict between our accepted policy of freedom of speech and press and our national security needs. Long-range questions regarding freedom of information include:

Just what information should be published and available to the public?

Should more of this information be published, accessible, or classified, and if so, by whom?

Do we want only the government to publish it or does the private sector have the right to publish it also?

Who should pay for this information?

Do citizens have the right to see every detail of their government's actions?

When is secrecy legitimate?

These are just a few of the social and legal implications of the United States government as a publisher of important and often sensitive information. The depository system provides for a tremendous amount of free access to the information published, but it is not without its problems and faults. Students should be encouraged to use government information actively and critically.

Sample Learning Objectives

Concepts to understand:

The Federal Depository Library Act.

The nature, types, and uses of government publications.

How and why access to government publications differs from other library materials.

Major access sources for government publications.

Issues related to the access of government information.

The potential for bias and alteration in government publications.

Skills to apply:

Identifying and locating government publications on a subject.

Critically evaluating government publications.

Sample Class Discussion Questions

1. What is a government publication?
2. How many of you have ever used government documents?
3. If you have not used government documents, why not?
4. Why do you suppose government publications are important?

5. Where can you find government publications?
6. What is the Federal Depository Act?
7. How can you determine what government publications are available on a particular subject?
8. What are some types of government publications?
9. How might you use government publications in your research? In your personal life? In your professional life?
10. What is the Freedom of Information Act?
11. What is classified information?
12. Why has government information become more limited in recent years?
13. Should government information be available for commercial publication?
14. What are the risks of open access to government information?
15. What are the risks of restricted access to government information?
16. Do you think bias is a problem in government publications?

Sample In-Class Activities

1. Students visit a government documents department or hear a presentation by a government documents librarian.
2. Students browse through an array of government publications.
3. Students read up on and debate one of the social or legal implications of government publishing.
4. In small groups, students make brief oral reports on one of the social or legal implications of government publications.
5. As a class, students describe a society in which there is no access to government information.

Sample Take-Home Exercises

1. Students identify and locate government publications on a topic.
2. Students critically evaluate a government publication or access tool.
3. Students find and compare a book or periodical article on a subject with a government publication on the same subject.

Notes and Suggested Reading

1. Laurence Schmeckebier, *Government Publications and Their Use* (Washington, D.C.: Brookings Institute, 1969).

2. Patrick J. Wilkinson, "Potential Technological and Institutional Barriers to U.S. Government Information," *RQ* 26:425–433 (Summer 1987).

Chapter 15

Information Policy
and Politics

Charlotta C. Hensley

Information is power; politics is about access to and use of power. Information policy is, therefore, political in that it attempts to define
who has access to power (information). What is published, by whom,
and for which audience are facets of the policies and politics of information in the United States. The concept of knowledge and information as power was recognized by the framers of the U.S. Constitution,
whose intent was to empower each citizen through speech, writing,
publishing, and access to information. How freely and equally citizens
have access to information determines how freely and equally gover-
nance is shared. U.S. government policy prescribes freedom of speech
and access to information for each citizen, but its uneven implementation in publishing practices has omitted some voices, such as those of
women, and has consequently led to a major increase in independent
publishing since the early 1970s.

U.S. Information Policy

In the United States, the politics of information is established by the
social policies of the federal government concerning citizen production
of and access to information. Policy has its root meaning in the Greek
politēs (citizen) and is a course of action adopted and pursued by an individual or agency. Information can be viewed as the dynamic act of
informing. Information policy in the United States is intended to produce an active, informed citizenry.

Charlotta Hensley has been at the University of Colorado, Boulder, Libraries since 1969;
she is currently Assistant Director for Research and Development and Women Studies
Bibliographer.

The First Amendment to the Constitution of the United States declares that "Congress shall make no law...abridging the freedom of speech or of the press...." The intent of this amendment concerning citizen production of and access to information is elaborated in James Madison's draft version of the speech and press clauses, introduced in the House of Representatives on June 8, 1789: "The people shall not be deprived or abridged of their right to speak, to write, or to publish their sentiments; and the freedom of the press, as one of the great bulwarks of liberty, shall be inviolable."[1] Clearly, freedom of speech for citizens in the United States includes not only oration but also the writing and dissemination of individual opinion. Expressing any viewpoint, popular or unpopular, by speaking, writing, or publishing is a social right granted by the framers and adopters of the Constitution. Diversity of opinion is, however, among the most controversial rights of U.S. citizenship.

Domestic intellectual property laws concerning copyright and patents are also based on the Constitution of the United States and are intended to encourage authors to disseminate their work publicly. Article I, Section 8 grants Congress the authority to enact copyright and patent legislation in order to "promote the Progress of Science and useful Arts, by securing for limited Times to Authors and Inventors the exclusive Right to their respective Writings and Discoveries." This passage provided the rationale for the first Copyright Act (1790) and for all subsequent revisions. The traditional purpose of constitutional copyright authorization is explicit; for example, in the 1909 Act:

> The enactment of copyright legislation by Congress under the terms of the Constitution is not based on any natural right that the author has in his writings, for the Supreme Court has held that such rights...are purely statutory rights, but on the ground that the welfare of the public will be served and progress of science and useful arts will be promoted....Not primarily for the benefit of the author, but primarily for the benefit of the public such rights are given. Not that any particular class of citizens, however worthy, may benefit, but because the policy is believed to be for the benefit of the great body of people, in that it will stimulate writing and invention to give some bonus to authors and inventors.[2]

U.S. information policy is implemented through both the public education (or literacy) of citizens and a system of information creation, publishing, and access involving individuals, publishers, and librarians. Individuals create information for the public domain by speaking and by writing, which might be disseminated by either private or public publication. Public access to written information and knowledge has traditionally been supported by citizen contribution to education and to libraries through taxation. Constraints on the freedom of speech may be legal, economic, or social, all of which impinge on information policy.

Information in the United States

CREATION

Information is created primarily by individuals or groups privately or in academic, corporate, or government institutions. Types of writing normally include literary works, descriptions of discoveries, and syntheses of existing information into differing interpretations. The intent is to provide society with imaginative work and factual information for its use.

PUBLICATION

Whether information is publicly disseminated depends on its publication by either profit-making ("trade") or nonprofit publishers. Decisions about trade publishing involve the marketability of the author and topic as well as the costs of author payments and royalties, printing, advertising, and distribution in relationship to the profit to be made. Since public access to and use of printed material are practically impossible to monitor, profit margins for trade publishers have traditionally been small, involving a single charge at the time of purchase and little control of its users. Librarians, for example, buy books for anonymous patrons to read many times without further charge to the library by publishers.

Rapidly developing technology is challenging these traditional publishing and intellectual property assumptions. Electronic formats are accelerating a change from many small U.S. trade publishers to a few multinational conglomerates whose officers view themselves as owners of information.[3] Because online databases often are unique and are accessible from multiple sites, and because CD-ROM publishers license rather than sell their products, pricing policies are based on multiple uses of the information instead of on the traditional costs (paper, printing, postage) of producing a printed publication. Higher profits are assured because access to and use of information is more easily monitored when a work is controlled by the publisher, who is the only source of distribution.

Nonprofit publishing, therefore, is becoming more crucial to a balanced information policy and to an informed citizenry. Nonprofit publishers include local, state, and federal governments; learned societies, professional associations, and university presses; and thousands of small, independent publishers. Nonprofit publishing is generally supported by institutional (taxes, grants, subventions) or individual (donations) subsidies, so that information about topics or points of view not popular enough to make a profit in competitive publishing is nevertheless available.

The federal government is the largest nonprofit producer and publisher of information in the United States. Its policies concerning research and publication have enormous impact on citizen access to information. Widely available, inexpensive, and without copyright, federal publications have made people aware of government policies and programs while at the same time they have stimulated economic, educational, and scientific development. Should the traditional role of the federal government in information dissemination to citizens change, then the role of other nonprofit publishers will become even more crucial to implementing the ideal of free access to information.

Because trade publishing decisions are primarily based on marketability (a promulgation of popular opinion), diverse points of view held by minorities within the population often have not reached print. The number of independent publishers, however, has increased dramatically in the last twenty years, following a reidentification of the lack of access to traditional publishing outlets as a characteristic of such social movements as ethnic and women's rights. The second edition of the *International Directory of Little Magazines and Small Presses* (1966), for example, lists 822 independent publishers, while the twenty-fourth (1988–1989) includes more than 4,000. In order to provide direct, unrestricted commentary on social issues, independent nonprofit publishers often depend on the financial support and energy of volunteers. This type of publishing is vital to information policy in reflecting the diversity of viewpoint and background of the U.S. population.

ACCESS

Information is preserved for social use by libraries, which are supported by private or public funding to serve as depositories for the current and historical information, knowledge, wisdom, and creative endeavors required by the citizenry. Libraries are, then, important components in the achievement of information dissemination in the United States.

In acknowledging the role of libraries in U.S. information policy, the Council of the American Library Association has established basic policies for library services in its *Library Bill of Rights*. Individual librarians also subscribe to a code of ethics that reinforces the *Library Bill of Rights*. Although they acknowledge the ideal of providing access to all of the cumulated information of our society, librarians are restricted by budgets when developing their collections. Few public or academic librarians can afford to buy all the estimated 800,000 books or 108,000 serials titles available internationally each year, or the estimated 45,000 books and 61,000 serials published annually in the United States. Consequently, collection development policies emphasize primary library users and result in a focus on majority interests.

CONSTRAINTS

Social constraints placed on freedom of speech include the policies of the federal government concerning dissemination of its information to citizens, citizen participation in information policy, and censorship.

Federal government policies since 1980 concerning restrictions on publishing the information collected by its agencies, reliance on commercial organizations to publish government information, attempts to prevent open dissemination of the results of unclassified research at scientific meetings, and the FBI Library Awareness Program are cause for alarm and for the assertion that the Reagan administration has made the most systematic and broadbased attempt to manipulate information and curb dissent of any peacetime U.S. government.[4] In documenting reduced federal support for research about women, for example, Rubin points out that the "lack of available records about research in general and research on women since 1980 in particular effectively blocks the monitoring of public monies within several major agencies."[5]

Citizens control the success of information policy by tax support for education and libraries, which is influenced by their information requirements and by their opinions about the method of access to it. Of concern is the high rate of illiteracy and nonreading among the adult population in the United States. According to Kozol, one-third of adults cannot read above a ninth-grade level and therefore obtain information only from associates, friends, radio, or television.[6] An illiterate population has little interest in supporting libraries. Of American adults, 45 percent do not read newspapers, affecting their concept of freedom of the press. In a 1987 survey of public familiarity with the Constitution, for example, 61 percent thought a constitutional convention should be convened to reconsider the first amendment.[7] As technology improves electronic access to information, individual convenience and ability to pay for information access from homes and offices could affect support for libraries, which provide access to information for the general citizenry.

Citizen toleration of all points of view is tenuous. Surveys consistently indicate that the majority of the U.S. public does not favor censorship, but attempts to control what people say and read have increased in the past decade.[8] Although motivation for citizen attempts to restrict access to information varies, there continues to be discomfort with the freedom of speech, writing, and publishing granted by U.S. information policies. Areas particularly focused upon by censors include religion, minority rights, and literature and instructional material for young readers.

Beliefs and practices that differ from those of the majority in a community are often controversial. In July 1986, for example, members of local Christian churches attempted to prevent a San Jose (California) Public Library program featuring Z Budapest, a Dianic Wicca practitioner, although 700 people attended.[9] *Our Bodies, Ourselves*, a book about women's health and sexuality, became a focus for a national call from a group that wanted access to it limited in public and school libraries.[10]

Concern about the ideas to which young people are exposed is perhaps the most common rationale for censorship in U.S. public schools and libraries. Limitations placed on instructional and library materials include precensorship as well as challenges to already selected material. Precensorship involves policies that preclude the selection of material for classrooms or libraries. The Texas State Textbook Committee, which selects texts for public schools in the state, has been shown to have been unduly influenced by two people.[11] Because Texas is the second largest purchaser of textbooks in the United States, textbook publishers often follow the Texas criteria for content, thereby limiting the options of teachers throughout the rest of the country. Policies for selecting library materials might also be construed as precensorship if librarians emphasize only a single criterion, such as the values of the majority in a community, in order to avoid controversy.

Accusations of precensorship are leveled not only at people who represent traditional values but also at those who represent "liberal" values. Phyllis Schlafly, for example, writes the following:

Like the thief who cries "Stop, thief" in order to distract attention from his own crime, the liberals are crying "censorship" to try to hide the fact that *they* are the most ruthless censors of all. The list is endless of the topics and books which the liberals have censored out of the school curriculum, out of school and public libraries, and out of the media. Here are a few examples:

1. The physical dangers and disadvantages of promiscuity (especially to girls) and the incurability of venereal herpes.
2. The phonics method of teaching first-graders to read, including all authentic real-phonics first-grade readers and work books.
3. Prayer and all references to God and our American religious heritage in public schools.
4. The evidence that the earth was created rather than evolved, and that it may *not* be millions of years old.
5. Factual information which shows that the American private enterprise system has produced more material abundance than any other economic system in the history of the world.
6. Factual evidence, ever since 1967, which proves the growing military superiority of the Soviet Union over the United States.
7. Words, pictures and concepts that might lead little girls to want to be fulltime, career homemakers when they grow up, instead of dedicating their lives to the paid labor force.
8. The facts about how Federal tax funds are used to finance special-interest groups, especially women's lib groups.
9. The facts about how "women's studies" courses at colleges and universities teach anti-family concepts and lesbianism.
10. The arguments against the Equal Rights Amendment, showing why ERA was defeated over a ten-year period despite massive propaganda in its behalf.[12]

A second form of censorship is challenges to material already selected. These might come from parents who do not want their children exposed to specific instructional or library materials; from school administrators, librarians, staff, students, or trustees; from organized groups; or from individual members of the community. An eleven-year study of one school district revealed that from 119 reconsideration requests received, 22 books were removed from libraries. Reasons included racism, sexism, religion, sex, violence, and profanity.[13] Censorship attempts in schools and libraries reflect not only individual and community values but also a view that the purpose of educating youth is to teach a prescribed body of knowledge rather than to develop an ability to think critically about social issues.

A Case Study: Feminist Publishing

One result of the resurgence of interest in the equality and rights of women in the 1970s, the second wave of feminism in the United States, was the recognition that a characteristic of oppressed social groups is the lack of access to traditional publishing ("Freedom of the press belongs to those who own the presses"). Consequently, there has been a passionate feminist commitment to independent publishing, and often the first major purchase of an organization was a mimeograph machine. The growth in the number of feminist publishers has been phenomenal, from a few in the early 1970s to more than 111 women's presses and publishers, 11 women's news services, and 702 women's periodicals in 1989.[14]

The objectives of independent feminist publishing are to overcome the past silences of women by providing a place for their writing; to maintain the movement by providing a forum for the exchange of ideas and perspectives; and to effect cultural, economic, and political change. Its characteristics include control of content by using volunteer contributions and labor for the costs of publishing and distribution. An example is this plea from the publishers of *Hurricane Alice*:

> This summer, the editors had to begin to compute the value of the time we give, in order to figure our in-kind income for a grant proposal. It amounts to...about $60,000 a year. Yet we produce the review for...between five and six thousand dollars. How do we do it? We pay only for production. Supporters... give the rest in-kind: office space, overhead, clerical support, supplies, travel expenses, and the work of planning, selecting, editing, proofreading, and putting together.[15]

Inadequate funding, inexpensive formats, uneven content, irregular publication schedules, low circulation, and abbreviated publishing spans are often the result.

Independent feminist publishing often presents selection, access, and preservation challenges to librarians. Although feminist materials are relatively inexpensive, overhead costs may be more than those of trade publications. Identification is difficult because they are seldom reviewed in standard sources. Providing public access to them is problematic, since cataloging is rarely available in bibliographic databases, requiring local control. Of fifty-five active feminist spirituality periodicals identified in 1987, for example, only twenty-nine (53 percent) were found in the OCLC database, with twenty-one (38 percent) having ISSNs and Library of Congress cataloging. Indexing is also limited; only seven (13 percent) of the fifty-five titles appeared in indexes.[16] Since many feminist publications are for women only, serious questions about restricted access are raised for librarians in institutions using public funds to acquire, process, and provide service for them. Some publications, especially those about sexuality, risk censorship by mutilation or theft when shelved openly. Special collections of feminist materials involve nonstandard bibliographic control and limited public access, although questions of publisher-controlled circulation and materials protection are eased. Inexpensive formats, such as newsprint, and the unavailability of commercial microformats require local preservation solutions.

Since feminist publications are, however, often at the forefront of women's cultural and theoretical expression, they are important resources for contemporary ideas, issues of concern, and individual expression through which women may gain a sense of community. They are also primary sources for research. Their inherent challenges in acquiring, providing access to, protecting, and preserving them are not appropriate reasons for excluding them from academic or public library collections. They are examples of materials traditionally excluded from mainstream publishing and library collections, and their exclusion has resulted in the abrogation of the right of U.S. citizens to write, to publish, and thereby to share their sentiments.

Sample Learning Objectives

Concepts to understand:

> The nature and development of information policy in the United States.
> The significance and growth of nonprofit publishing.
> The social responsibility of U.S. libraries to provide access to information.
> Constraints to the freedom of speech.
> The uneven results vis-à-vis diverse points of view of the social practice of U.S. information policy.
> The development of feminist publishing.

Skills to apply:

As this is a content rather than skills-based unit, no applications other than a relevant guest speaker and in-class discussion are suggested.

Sample Class Discussion Questions

1. What role do libraries play in U.S. information policy?
2. What are the pros and cons of restricting access to material in libraries? What are the implications for an author? For society? For the librarian?
3. Should the marketplace decide what is actually published? What would the consequences be? If not the marketplace, who or what should determine what is published?
4. Should authors and publishers have more control over the uses made of their intellectual work? Why and why not?

Sample In-Class Activity

This chapter was written by a guest speaker in my course, and this guest speaker approach is highly recommended. Potential guest speakers include an independent, alternative publisher; a librarian or school teacher who has been involved in a censorship case; a lawyer involved with intellectual freedom; or a representative of the American Civil Liberties Union or the Moral Majority.

Notes

1. *Annals of Congress*, 1st Cong., 434.

2. *Intellectual Property Rights in an Age of Electronics and Information: Summary* (Washington, D.C.: U.S. Congress Office of Technology Assessment, April 1986), p. 7.

3. Robert Maxwell, *Global Business* 1:41 (Spring 1988).

4. Donna Demac, *Liberty Denied* (New York: PEN American Center, 1988).

5. Mary Rubin, "A Declining Federal Commitment to Research about Women, 1980-1984" (New York: National Council for Research on Women, 1986), p. 1.

6. Jonathan Kozol, *Illiterate America* (Garden City, N.Y.: Anchor Press–Doubleday, 1985).

7. James Kilpatrick, "Constitution Is Misunderstood," Boulder *Daily Camera*, Monday, Mar. 2, 1987, p. A6.

8. Howard White, "Majorities for Censorship," *Library Journal* 111:32 (July 1986).

9. *American Libraries* 17:503 (July–Aug. 1986).

10. *Library Acquisitions: Practice and Theory* 5:121–145 (1981).

11. "The Textbook Selection Process in Texas," *Interracial Books for Children Bulletin* 14:14–21 (1983).

12. Phyllis Schlafly, "Censorship—Real and Phony," *The Phyllis Schlafly Report* 16:1 (Feb. 1983).

13. Agnes Stahlschmidt, "A Workable Strategy for Dealing with Censorship," *Phi Delta Kappan* 64:99–101 (Oct. 1982).

14. Martha Leslie Allen, ed., *1989 Directory of Women's Media* (Washington, D.C.: Women's Institute for Peace and Freedom, 1989), cover.

15. Martha Roth, Letter to *Hurricane Alice* subscribers, 1985.

16. Charlotta C. Hensley, " 'Womanspirit' and Other Issues of Feminist Spirituality," *Serials Review* 13:6 (Spring 1987).

Suggested Reading

Coalition on Government Information Newsletter. Volume 1, 1987–   .

Danky, James P. and Elliot Shores, eds. *Alternative Materials in Libraries*. Metuchen, N.J.: Scarecrow, 1982.

Demac, Donna A. *Liberty Denied: The Current Rise of Censorship in America*. New York: PEN American Center, 1988.

Freedom to Read Foundation News. Volume 1, 1971–   .

Intellectual Property Rights in an Age of Electronics and Information. Washington, D.C.: U.S. Congress Office of Technology Assessment, 1986.

Newsletter on Intellectual Freedom. Volume 1, 1952–   .

Chapter 16

The Assimilation and
Application of Information

Four discrete stages are discernible in the overall research process: exploration and planning, data collection, assimilation, and application or communication. Just as background information must be gathered, vocabulary control established, and a search strategy developed before efficient and effective data gathering can be accomplished, the information collected must be absorbed and synthesized before it can be effectively communicated.

Writing, of course, is a complex, progressively developed skill. Many books and courses are dedicated to the improvement of writing. It is not within the scope of this guide or the course it suggests to cover writing skills. Therefore, no in-class or take-home assignments are included in this chapter. However, just as previous chapters go beyond the use of sources to their evaluation, this chapter goes beyond data gathering to the effective analysis of information in order to communicate a unique perspective.

Preparing to Write the First Draft

At the conclusion of data gathering, but before beginning to write the report, researchers should allow time to assimilate the information gathered: responding to notes, filling in gaps, developing a final outline and thesis, considering a title, and applying creative problem-solving techniques to stimulate a fresh approach. In this process, the researcher appropriates information and transforms it into a personal statement. Several of the same techniques and skills that improve library use will also enhance assimilation. For example, it may be useful to develop a writing strategy and timeline specifically for the assimilation and application stages.

Although students should consider and record their personal reactions to information throughout the research process, responses developed at this point will be the culmination of knowledge gained as a result of the entire process. For the best results, researchers will be relaxed and open, perhaps playful, as they review the data collected and allow their responses, thoughts, and ideas to arise. In such a state, students are more likely to evoke new insights, which can be recorded on cards. Another way to creatively tap innermost thoughts is to review the cards at night and free associate in the morning to stimulate original ideas.

During this time, students should also continue critical evaluation, noting what information they have selected and whether it represents the spectrum of available perspectives. Students might list the possible viewpoints on the topic to make sure that all are represented. If the researcher's intention is to take a stand on the topic, a stronger case can be built by reflecting on and addressing alternative arguments. Students should do a bias check, making sure their own point of view is thoughtfully based on the evidence gathered rather than on preconceived, emotional, or simply unquestioned assumptions.

As they review and sort cards, researchers should look for gaps and ask whether any additional information is required. More forays into the library may be called for, but an eye should be kept on the timeline; drafting time should not be cut short. Students who resist writing may be tempted to extend the library search as a delay tactic.

Researchers should also read through all note cards to confirm or develop the arrangement. If the preliminary outline has held up well, the researcher will find that the cards conform to the established organization. If the outline is no longer satisfactory, the notes themselves may suggest some type of order, or the student can experiment with standard approaches, such as chronological, cause and effect, general to particular, particular to general, or point and counterpoint. The value of index cards will be evident as the student easily arranges and rearranges all the cards or uses only the cards representing the main points.

Creative approaches are also useful for developing the final outline. Because the outline format is linear and sequential, many students find that it is not a comfortable vehicle for their thought patterns; a freeform or visual approach may be more suitable. In addition to mindmapping and clustering, described in chapter 5, any visual representation of concepts and points may be stimulating. Students can connect words and phrases with circles, boxes, lines, arrows, and even fanciful shapes to form patterns that may be abstract diagrams or pictorial representations. The result is the student's picture of the paper, which may suggest an organizational framework. If a formal outline is required, visual representation is also useful to generate the categories, points, and arrangement.

Over the course of the research process, a thesis statement may emerge through a series of adjustments and revisions, or it may burst forth fully formed in a moment of insight or revelation. A thesis is the author's stance or the whole point of the report in a single statement. The composition of the thesis may precede the development of the outline, which then becomes the logical extension of the thesis; or the thesis may result from the outline—its contraction into one statement. The thesis typically becomes the topic sentence of the first or second paragraph and is reiterated in the conclusion. By the time the thesis and outline have been crafted, a title is likely to suggest itself, although sometimes the title occurs as a final flourish.

Establishing the thesis, outline, and title may be useful warm-up exercises to prepare the student for the difficult task of beginning to write the first draft. Writing is seldom easy. Even the most practiced, prolific, and polished authors experience the inherent struggle and agony of the process. They also acknowledge the satisfaction of the craft, the thrill of creation, and the power of discovery. Just as library research is a process of discovery, so too is writing. What is understood about a subject will become deeper and more focused and will take on new dimensions as it is expressed and honed in writing.

Most research papers offer a synthesis, i.e., a unique composite of selected material and a considered perspective. If the scholarly literature conveys conversations among the experts, and library research provides the opportunity to tap into those discussions, then the research report communicates the essence of the student's conversations: what was heard as well as the student's responses.

In order to shape the pieces of information into a whole composition, the researcher studies the notes for themes, patterns, congruence, disparities, inconsistencies, and contradictions. What can the researcher reveal about the topic and how can it be presented for maximum impact? Creative problem-solving techniques may help to discover an aspect or viewpoint that has never been offered before, perhaps a paradigm or metaphor that provides a new way to relate to the subject. However, it is more important for assertions to be well-grounded than imaginative.

Writer's block is an experience common to both student and professional writers. There are numerous coping techniques. If time allows, the most simple solution is to walk away, leaving the paper for as long as possible. When that is not feasible, the student should work on another aspect of the report, perhaps reviewing notes or compiling the bibliography. The student might try brainstorming, free association, or visual representation. It is often useful to discuss the impasse with someone else, or coming back to the trouble point in the morning may provide a fresh perspective. Another technique is free writing: the student simply puts pen to paper or fingers to keyboard and writes anything at all for a specified period of time or number of pages.

Elements of Revising, Editing, and Proofreading

Some writers quickly sketch a loose, rough draft to capture all their thoughts and ideas in the order they occur, disregarding mechanics and development. This draft is then reworked and rewritten many times. Others prefer to ponder and polish each sentence and paragraph as it is written. In either case, the penultimate draft will require additional revisions, editing, and proofreading. Ideally, this draft will be set aside for as long as possible before revising. Writers often become attached to words and phrases that were particularly strenuous or delightful to conjure or compose: time provides detachment, which eases the editing process.

Revising focuses on the overall report and its major parts, editing is concerned with the smaller elements within the report, and proofreading examines details. These procedures are enormously facilitated by word processing. In fact, the student who writes with a word processor is more likely to engage in these activities throughout the writing process rather than to concentrate on them at the conclusion. Nevertheless, the procedures are the same for the typist or word processor, whether they are considered continuously or addressed at the end.

INTEGRITY

To revise, the student studies the complete draft for content and personal style. First the student will want to make sure all requirements have been met:

Have all conditions of the assignment been fulfilled?
Is the appropriate audience addressed?

Is the purpose of the report accomplished?
Is the thesis sustained?

Next the student can check for completeness, coherence, and flow:

Have all necessary points been made?
Does every point relate to the thesis and outline?
Does every paragraph relate to the relevant point?
Are transitions clear, logical, and structured to build the argument?
Is there a well-developed introduction, body, and conclusion?

QUOTATIONS

The student must determine whether there is an appropriate ratio of source and original material:

Does the report offer an original contribution or is it just an assemblage of the thoughts of others?
Do the number of quotations detract from the report's readability? Is every quotation apropos—is all quoted material best said in those particular words because they are so precise, well crafted, elegant, or original?
Is credit given for the original expressions or ideas of others?

OVERALL EFFECT

The student should also read the report for its overall effect:

Is the purpose fulfilled in a way that honestly represents the student?
Is a personal style apparent and appropriate?
Is the final result satisfying?

At this point, researchers could also adapt the questions from the four levels of critical evaluation in chapter 10 to assess their reports from the perspective of another reader.

STYLE MANUALS

In the editing phase, the report is examined closely for adherence to the conventions of standardized style, as set forth by the style manual selected at the outset of the research process. If an instructor does not require a particular style manual, students should ask which manual is preferred. There are both general style manuals, as published by the University of Chicago or the Modern Language Association, and discipline-based manuals, as published by the American Psychological Association or the American Chemical Society. The details of footnote and bibliographic form vary from manual to manual; also, some manuals provide more comprehensive guidelines than others. If the instructor declines to recommend a manual, a librarian may be able to help by recommending the most current or accessible manual available or the one used most frequently on campus.

As a general guideline, if students have a "funny feeling" about anything in the report at this point, they are probably right! Even if the solution is not immediately apparent, the troublesome item should be tagged and returned to until it is resolved. Another reader may more readily be able to suggest an alternative.

STYLE

Another series of questions can be posed about the report's written style:

> Is the tone suitable for the subject, the assignment, the audience, and the student's level of expertise?
>
> Is the language clear and appropriate? Are all words used correctly, do they convey what is intended, do they portray bias? In addition to emotionally charged or value-laden terms, students should be on the alert for words with sexist or racist connotations. Most students will be aware that many people react to the generic masculine pronoun, for example. To determine the importance of nonsexist language, students should consider the negative effect such language may have on their audience and whether that will detract from their purpose.
>
> Are the sentence structures, grammar, spelling, and punctuation correct?
>
> Do footnotes and bibliography conform exactly to the specified style manual?

QUALITY OF EXPRESSION

A very effective technique to check quality of expression is to read the report out loud, or, even better, to have it read out loud to the writer. The student will listen for clear, crisp, well-crafted prose, asking:

Is each thought cleanly, clearly developed?
Is the expression of content explicit and varied?
Does every sentence relate to the paragraph it is in?
Is every word necessary to develop the sentence it is in?

In completing the final draft, students should check the assignment one last time to be sure all required parts are included, such as a title page, contents or outline, endnotes, and bibliography.

PROOFREADING

For many of the functions described thus far, software aids have been developed; programs are available to assist in generating ideas, developing outlines, organizing content, and checking syntax, grammar, spelling, punctuation, and other elements of style. Computerized revising and editing are noncontextual and far from absolute, however; the final proofreading always remains the full responsibility of the author.

The very last step is to be sure that all intentions have been transmitted to the final draft. Once again the student reads for spelling, punctuation, footnote and bibliographic form, and especially typographic errors. Having invested the massive effort required to plan, research, and write a report, the student should convey not final carelessness, but sustained thoughtfulness and achievement in the ultimate product.

Sample Learning Objectives

Concepts to understand:

The importance of taking time to respond to notes.
The process of developing a final outline, thesis, and title.
The research report as synthesis and creative response.
The nature and importance of revising, editing, and proofreading.

Sample Class Discussion Questions

1. Can you identify four basic stages in the research process?
2. What steps should follow data collection but precede writing the first draft?

3. How can you stimulate responses to your notes?
4. How can you determine whether your notes are well-balanced?
5. What should you do if you discover gaps in your notes?
6. If the preliminary outline is no longer appropriate, how can you develop a final outline?
7. How is a final thesis developed?
8. What are your feelings about writing?
9. What is a synthesis?
10. What creative problem-solving techniques can be used to ease writing?
11. What is a style manual? How is it used in the research process?
12. Why is it important to avoid emotionally charged and value-laden terms?
13. What should be considered in the revision process?
14. What should editing include?
15. What should you look for in proofreading?
16. Why is proofreading so important?

Index

Deborah Fink is the instructional services librarian for the University of Colorado Libraries. She has published several articles, including "Information Technology and Library Research" in *Conceptual Frameworks for Bibliographic Education: Theory into Practice*. She also has served as co-editor of "BI Line: A Column on Bibliographic Instruction" in *Colorado Libraries*. Fink received her MLS from the University of California–Los Angeles.